EXPLODING THE MYTHS
THAT COULD DESTROY AMERICA

EXPLODING THE MYTHS THAT COULD DESTROY AMERICA

BY

ERWIN W. LUTZER

MOODY PRESS

CHICAGO

Library of Congress Cataloging-in-Publication Data

Lutzer, Erwin W.
Exploding the myths that could destroy America.

1. United States—Moral conditions.   2. Christian
ethics.   I. Title.
HN90.M6L87   1986   306′.0973   85-29665
ISBN 0-8024-5692-8 (pbk.)

6 7 Printing/LC/Year 88

With affection, to the members and
friends of the Moody Church,
Whose love and prayers have
been a continual encouragement to
me and my family
And whose lives are salt and light
in our decaying society

CONTENTS

CHAPTER   PAGE

Foreword   9

1. The Myth That the Battle Isn't Real   11

2. The Myth That Life Began with
Blind Chance   27

3. The Myth That We Can Have Morality
Without Religion   45

4. The Myth That Whatever Is Legal
Is Moral   61

5. The Myth That Morality Cannot Be
Legislated   77

6. The Myth That the Roles of Men and
Women Are Interchangeable   91

7. The Myth That a Fetus Is Not a Baby   107

8. The Myth That We Can Ignore the
Ghost of Karl Marx   123

9. The Myth That Pornography Is a
Harmless Adult Pleasure   143

10. The Myth That the Church Should Have
No Voice in Government   159

11. The Myth That We Can Take on Water
and Stay Afloat   173

12. The Myth That We Can Win the War
Without Sacrifice   189

FOREWORD

Pastor Erwin W. Lutzer is among only six persons (including Francis Schaeffer, Frank Gabelein, and Josh McDowell) to have received the honorary LL.D. degree from The Simon Greenleaf School of Law: he is almost unique among incumbents of great American metropolitan pulpits in combining theological depth with dynamic attention to current issues. His latest book, *Exploding the Myths That Could Destroy America,* is a hard hitting exposé of the ideological, secularist nonsense that can only weaken our nation. Read it to learn how to do a proper job of "demythologizing"—not in the manner of a Rudolf Bultmann, who excised the miraculous from biblical revelation, but with the maturity of an Erwin Lutzer, who uses the sharp edge of God's living and written Word to cut down the shibboleths in contemporary society.

DR. JOHN WARWICK MONTGOMERY
M.Phil. in Law (Essex), Ph.D. (Chicago),
Th.D. (Strasbourg)
of the Middle Temple, Barrister-at-Law
Dean, The Simon Greenleaf School of Law,
Anaheim, California, and Strasbourg, France

1

THE MYTH THAT
THE BATTLE ISN'T REAL

A reporter asked a pedestrian, "Do you know what the two greatest problems in America are?"

"I don't know, and I don't care!" the man responded.

"Then you've got both of them!" was the abrupt reply.

Although our nation is rotting on the inside and hostile forces are determined to take away our freedom, our greatest problem might just be that there are too many people who neither know nor care. Not until all is lost will many awake to the painful reality that America as we once knew it is gone. Because the transition is happening over a period of years, millions don't realize it is happening at all.

In John Bunyan's classic work *The Holy War* the fortress is besieged by strong malignant forces, but these enemies cannot capture the fortress until its gates are opened from the inside. Do you remember the discussion of how the fortress would eventually be overrun? Diabolus speaking to his cohorts says, "We'll cajole them, delude them, pretending things that will never be and promising things they shall never get. Lies, lies, lies—the only way to get Mansoul to let us in."[1]

Throughout history, nations, like people, have frequently fallen victim to lies—myths that become accepted as truth. How these myths begin makes little difference. But once they are disseminated they are difficult to combat because the populace seems eager to believe them. When uncontested, the myths take over.

In George Orwell's *1984* we have a compelling description of how the so-called Ministry of Truth used *Newspeak* to brainwash the people of Oceania. The party slogans were WAR IS PEACE; FREEDOM IS SLAVERY; IGNORANCE IS STRENGTH. Through crafty manipulation, these lies were eventually believed.

The same technique is used in America today. Subtly, if not overtly, myths are sold to the American public. Daily through television, the newspapers, and the decisions of the courts we are bombarded with a certain understanding of the way things ought to be. These assumptions are often presented uncritically, giving the impression that no thoughtful person would contest their validity. Yet they are as misleading as the slogans in Orwell's book.

Will Herberg, a Jewish scholar who taught at Drew University, once observed that the brainwashing we receive daily from our cultural environment is far more deadly than any rational arguments from atheists.

Myths are subtly being forced upon us. If we accept them we will buy our ticket to repression and intolerance. And once the train is rolling, we've got no choice as to where we're headed. Those decisions are made for us by the self-styled engineers who plead for pluralism as they simultaneously lobby for

1. Ethel Barrett, *Chronicles of Mansoul* (Glendale, Calif.: Regal, 1980), p. 5.

laws that would deny freedom to everyone except themselves. They not only want complete control of the train but want to force everyone to get on board. The more widely their myths are believed, the more pressure there is for everyone to get moving in the same direction.

THE SOURCE OF THE MYTHS

And where might these myths have originated? In one sense they are as old as the Garden of Eden, where Satan convinced Eve that if she disobeyed the Almighty she could rule her own life. She could be her own god and escape thoughtless dependency on a Being who had no claim to her life in the first place. In fact, Satan told her that, if she disobeyed, she herself would be like God, knowing good and evil.

Through the centuries these conflicting viewpoints have vied for supremacy. In our day the argument turns on the debate between humanism and the Judeo-Christian world view. Today, as back then, the dispute continues: *Will mankind be ruled by God, or is he capable of ruling himself?*

The word *humanism* has crept into our vocabulary during recent years. But what is it? Is it really a threat to our freedom as some Christians assert? Some writers try to minimize the conflict between Christianity and humanism by suggesting that humanism is perfectly compatible with a reasonable interpretation of Christianity and that only religious extremists (such as the Moral Majority) would suggest otherwise. As David Bollier wrote, "To most Americans the term *humanism* simply conjures up images of academic study ("The Humanities" or cultural refinement and sensibilities)."[2] He points out that humanism as tradi-

2. David Bollier, "The Witchhunt Against Secular Humanism," *Humanist* 44(September/October 1984):12.

tionally understood is in harmony with the likes of Aquinas and Erasmus. He argues that those who criticize humanism as anti-Christian are attacking a straw man erected by intolerant bigots who are ignorant of history. These extremists simply want to rid America of the pluralism that made it great. Bollier's book *Liberty and Justice for Some* expands the same argument. "Respected mainstream theologians reject the false dichotomy that pits 'humanism' against Christianity (as understood by ultrafundamentalists . . . although ultrafundamentalists consider 'Christian humanism' to be a contradiction in terms, the doctrine is in fact a respected discipline in the Christian church stretching back to St. Thomas Aquinas."[3]

But does the word *humanism* refer simply to a study of the humanities as Bollier implies? Certainly that is one aspect of the word. Studies such as art, literature, music, and philosophy, which are the products of human creativity, are listed under the Humanities section of the university's catalog. No serious-minded Christian is opposed to such studies but considers them necessary for a well-rounded education. Creativity is, after all, God-endowed, and we should not only study it, but Christians should be eager to contribute toward these disciplines.

But the word *humanism* has the same diversity of meaning as the word *religion*. Just as there are radically different religions, so humanism has various shades of meaning. Contemporary humanism traces its origin to the Renaissance, when there was a revival of classical learning and with it a greater emphasis on man's part in the world. Although this in itself is not wrong, as humanism progressed it diminished the need for God in the minds of men. From this came atheistic, or secular, humanism as expounded in the

3. David Bollier, *Liberty and Justice for Some* (New York: Frederick Unger, 1982), p. 99.

Humanist Manifestos I and II. In one sense secular humanism has been around throughout the history of philosophy as far back as 400 B.C., when Protagoras made his famous statement, "Man is the measure of all things."

Perhaps the best definition of secular humanism was given by Sir Julian Huxley, one of the founders of the American Humanist Association.

> I use the word "humanist" to mean someone who believes that man is just as much a natural phenomenon as an animal or plant; that his body, mind and soul were not supernaturally created but are products of evolution, and that he is not under the control or guidance of any supernatural being or beings, but has to rely on himself and his own power.[4]

In this book the word *humanism* will refer to the beliefs explained in *The Humanist Manifesto* and *A Secular Humanist Declaration.* These views, known as secular humanism, are based on an atheistic view of the world and the belief that evolution, operating independently of any transcendent powers, accounts for life as we know it. The author, Paul Kurtz, explains, "We can discover no divine purpose or providence for the human species . . . no deity will save us; we must save ourselves . . . promises of immortal salvation or fear of eternal damnation are both illusionary and harmful."[5]

BUILDING BLOCKS OF SECULAR HUMANISM

ATHEISM

Secular humanism embraces many different philosophical perspectives, but the common thread is the

4. Quoted by Henry M. Morris, *Education for the Real World* (San Diego: Creation Life, 1977), p. 82.
5. Paul Kurtz, ed., *Humanist Manifestos I and II* (New York: Prometheus, 1973), p. 16.

belief that there is no God. "Secular humanists may be agnostics, atheists, rationalists, or skeptics, but they find insufficient evidence for the claim that some divine purpose exists for the universe. They reject the idea that God has intervened miraculously in history or revealed Himself to a chosen few, or that He can save or redeem sinners."[6]

EVOLUTION

"Modern science discredits such historic concepts as a 'ghosts in the machine' and the 'separable soul.' Rather, science affirms that the human species is an emergence from natural evolutionary forces. As far as we know, the total personality is a function of the biological organism transacting in a social and cultural context. There is no credible evidence that life survives the death of the body."[7]

MORAL RELATIVISM

"We affirm that moral values derive their source from human experience. Ethics is autonomous and situational, needing no theological or ideological sanction."[8]

FREEDOM OF INQUIRY

"To enhance freedom and dignity the individual must experience a full range of *civil liberties* in all societies. This includes freedom of speech and press, political democracy, the legal right of opposition to governmental policies, fair judicial process, religious liberty, freedom of association, and artistic, scientific,

6. Paul Kurtz, *A Secular Humanist Declaration* (New York: Prometheus, 1980), p. 18.
7. Kurtz, *Humanist Manifestos*, pp. 16-17.
8. Ibid., p. 17.

and cultural freedom. It also includes a recognition of an individual's right to die with dignity, euthanasia, and the right to suicide."[9]

ONE WORLD GOVERNMENT

"We deplore the division of humankind on nationalistic grounds. We have reached a turning point in human history where the best option is to transcend the limits of national sovereignty and to move toward the building of a world community in which all sectors of the human family can participate. Thus we look to the development of a system of world law and a world order based on transnational federal government."[10]

Is THE BATTLE REAL?

Obviously the beliefs of secular humanism are not new. So why should they receive so much attention in America today? Since humanism and Christianity have coexisted in the United States for more than two hundred years, we might think that they could live peaceably for many years to come. But there are powerful reasons to suggest that this is impossible. As humanism gains in strength it becomes more intolerant and will eventually crush religious freedom.

That humanism stands in direct opposition to Christianity is clear enough. But, as suggested, we might think it is possible for these beliefs to coexist with Christianity in America. After all, humanists say they are committed to pluralism, tolerance, and free inquiry. If this were so, Christianity would have nothing to fear.

But as welcome as such a prospect might be, humanism cannot grant Christianity a home within its

9. Ibid., p. 19.
10. Ibid., p. 21.

sanctuary. Its premises make such a truce impossible. The humanists' belief in moral relativism, government control, the cheapness of human life, and a materialistic view of reality are sharply in opposition to moral absolutes, the dignity of man, and religious freedom. *Humanism is not passive; it cannot indefinitely be tolerant of religion.* Paul Blanchard speaks for the militant attitude of humanists when he says:

> We have an obligation to expose and attack the world of religious miracles, magic, Bible-worship, salvationism, heaven, hell, and all mythical deities. We should be particularly specific and energetic in attacking such quack millennialists as Billy Graham and such embattled reactionaries as (the Pope) because they represent the two greatest anti-humanist aggregates in our society.[11]

The reason Christianity and humanism have been able to exist side by side in America is because this nation originally had what could be called a "Christian consensus" with its belief in human freedom, the dignity of all mankind, and morality. Thus America has had a tempered pluralism, in which differing points of view were accepted within a shared social perspective. But Richard Neuhaus, in his book *The Naked Public Square,* points out that pluralism cannot be maintained without shared moral discourse. As humanism moves farther away from Christian values, it will become increasingly intolerant of competing viewpoints. English historian E. R. Norman believed that "pluralism is a name that society gives itself when it is in the process of changing from one orthodoxy to another." This explains why those who speak most

11. Quoted by Kirby Anderson, "About Pluralism and Religion," *Dallas Morning News,* 22 October 1984.

loudly about the need for pluralism are often the most desirous of excluding religious values from the public arena. The freedoms that these champions of pluralism are fighting for are those that will deprive other people of their freedoms.

It is evident in the *Humanist Declaration* that humanism's professed belief in freedom of expression applies only to those views that are in keeping with its own understanding of the world. Though it professes belief in freedom of inquiry, a few pages later the authors write, "We deplore the efforts of fundamentalists (especially in the United States) to invade the science classrooms, requiring that creationist theory be taught to students and requiring that it be included in biology text books. This is a serious threat both to academic freedom and to the integrity of that educational process."[12] Freedom, then, for the humanist, does not mean that teachers should have freedom of speech; it means only freedom for humanistic dogma to be taught. Recent discoveries that disprove evolution will have to be suppressed.

Humanists frighten the public by extolling the evils of Europe when church and state were united. Heretics were burned at the stake, and scientists were condemned when their conclusions clashed with church dogma. This, they say, is what would happen in America if religion is not excluded from all influence in our schools and government. But of course evangelicals today do not advocate a return to the medieval belief that the state should be subject to the church. The reason the Pilgrims came to America was to worship in freedom without the interference of the state. But, more important, we should remember that the number of people who died under the hands of an intolerant church is minute in comparison to the num-

12. Kurtz, *A Secular Humanist Declaration*, p. 21.

ber who have died under the hands of intolerant humanistic states.

According to some estimates, Chairman Mao of China is credited with the death of 30 million Chinese; Stalin 30-60 million Russians, and Hitler 15 million people, of which 6 million were Jews. These figures do not include the multiplied millions who died in Viet Nam, Cambodia, and Hungary. What do all these deaths have in common? These people were killed because of the belief that there are no religious values, just relative ones. They died because they were considered to be animals, the product of blind evolutionary forces; they were massacred because the state believed that matter is the final reality, hence there is no God, no immortality, no final judgment. God was dethroned and the state was put in its place. As Dostoevski once wrote, "If God did not exist, everything would be permitted."[13]

In accepting the Templeton prize for Progress in Religion, Aleksandr Solzhenitsyn stated, "If I were asked today to formulate as concisely as possible the main cause of the ruinous revolution that swallowed up some 60 million of our people, I could not put it more accurately than to repeat: 'Men have forgotten God; that's why all this has happened.' "[14] An atheistic state will be as brutal as the evolutionary thesis upon which it is built, namely, the survival of the fittest. If personhood is only an oddity of chance and impersonal matter, there can be no human dignity, no value to human freedom or life itself. Anyone who stands in the way of the goals of the secular state will be crushed. As Hitler asked: Why should we not be as cruel as nature?

---

13. Jean-Paul Sartre, *Existentialism and Humanism*, trans. Philip Mairet (London: Methuen, 1948), p. 33.
14. Carl F. H. Henry, *The Christian Mindset in a Secular Society* (Portland, Ore.: Multnomah, 1984), p. 94.

The secular state does not always come by revolution; it can also evolve when the public becomes accustomed to the idea that the only solution to society's problems is state control. The humanists' strategy is to exploit a problem in society and then condition people to believe that the answer lies with the federal government. In America, the news media plays an important role in this conditioning process.

For example, virtually every news story about poverty in America places the blame for it on Washington. In the dozens of times I have seen such an analysis, I cannot recall once hearing that some of the responsibility should be shared by the spiritual and moral behavior of people. Yet no government on earth can wipe out poverty as long as alcoholism, immorality, and drug abuse are practiced on a wide scale. Regardless of how much money is spent for public housing or the creation of jobs, children will starve while their parents indulge their lower appetites.

Let me be quick to say that the government must do whatever it can to help the poor, and in many instances poverty is not the result of personal failure—but there must be a recognition that such problems have a spiritual dimension. By solely blaming the American government, people are conditioned to believe that the state bears full responsibility for all the needs of society. The next step is to get people to believe that the answer to our economic and social difficulties is to have a socialistic state where the rich will be forced to share their wealth with the poor by the abolition of private property.

Even the problem of child abuse, which receives so much attention in our newspapers, is used by humanists to try to show that we must allow the government to have a more direct hand in the rearing of our children. Feminists argue that the rise of child abuse is proof that parents do not know how to raise their children. They extol the virtues of communist countries where children are reared by teachers who provide day care twenty-four hours a day if necessary.

Perhaps the clearest indication that we are moving in the direction of a secular state with its arbitrary morality and devaluation of human life is the *Roe* v. *Wade* decision of the Supreme Court in 1973. As Hitler redefined *personhood* so that Jews would be excluded from the protection of the law, so preborn babies have been reclassified as nonpersons for the convenience of women. Secularism's disrespect for human life becomes apparent when we realize that nearly 20 million unborn babies have been mercilessly killed in the United States.

As already indicated, teachers in our public schools must use curriculum that is prescribed and prepared by secularists. All other religious convictions must be set aside in deference to the god of humanism. As humanist John Dunphy said:

> I am convinced that the battle for humankind's future must be waged and won in the public school classrooms by teachers who correctly perceive their role as the proselytizers of a new faith: a religion of humanity . . . the classroom must and will become an arena of conflict between the old and the new—the rotting corpse of Christianity, together with all its adjacent evils and misery, and the new faith of humanism.[15]

The erosion of moral decency is evident throughout society. Once again, the media has contributed to the myth that premarital sex, extramarital sex, and homosexuality are on the same moral level as chastity, monogomy, and heterosexuality. Under the banner of "equality" homosexuals want their sexual mores

15. Anderson, "About Pluralism."

taught in our public schools as simply an alternate sexual preference. The Playboy philosophy that has influenced so much of our culture teaches that any and all forms of sexual expression are legitimate just as long as they are pleasurable. The goal of many sex education classes taught in our schools is to teach teenagers how to have sex without guilt and without having a baby.

Given the growing intolerance of humanism, it is doubtful whether this nation can survive as a democracy unless there is a return to absolutes, a belief in God, and morality. If, as Arnold Toynbee has said, democracy is a leaf from the book of Christianity, our freedoms are in jeopardy when the influence of Christianity is extinguished. It is the Judeo-Christian belief that influenced the founding of this country and its assertion that "all men are created equal and are endowed by their Creator with certain unalienable rights." Without a belief in the Creator and accompanying inalienable rights, democracy cannot exist. As B. F. Skinner understood so well, if a man is the product of evolution and hence evolved through the animal world, he has neither freedom nor dignity. Yet those are the two qualities that must be present for the survival of democracy.

In a smear campaign aimed at what Norman Lear calls "the new right," Christians have been painted in the same hues as the Nazis and the Ku Klux Klan. Because Christians believe in the freedoms that America has had for two hundred years, they are considered the lunatic fringe. Make no mistake about the intention of these secularists: It is to discredit the voice of Christians so that America will tolerate only *one* religion, secular humanism.

The Supreme Court acknowledged that humanism is a religion in the 1961 *Torcase* v. *Watkins* case, so the battle lines are between two religions: humanism and

Judeo-Christian beliefs. The religion of humanism sees Christianity as a threat to secularism, *and it is.* In those countries where secularization is complete, the state has tried to exterminate all religion. Clearly two world views are on a collision course.

If as Francis Schaeffer has said, humanism has now replaced Christianity as the consensus of the West, our freedom is in jeopardy. The myths of humanism could destroy America.

Perhaps it will come as a surprise that the pastor of a well-known evangelical church should address the topics raised in this book. After all, my primary responsibility as a minister is to preach the gospel. How can I justify writing a book dedicated to exposing the philosophical myths of humanism?

My calling is to preach the gospel in light of the trends around us. As Karl Barth rightly observed, the effective preacher is the one with the Bible in one hand and a newspaper in the other. In his book *Save America!* Edward Rowe asks why the Christians in Germany were oblivious to Hitler's methods and intentions. A Christian who lived through the war told Rowe, "Most of the Bible believing Christians of Germany were right on Hitler's bandwagon at the time of his rise to power . . . these Christians were so busy with their Bible studies, their prayer meetings, their worship services, and their Christian fellowship that they were almost totally unaware of the controlling realities of the time."[16]

America is, as Elton Trueblood has said, "the cut-flower generation." We still have the semblance of life because of the momentum of the past. But if we are cut off from the source of life, we will eventually wither and die.

16. Ron Jenson, *Together We Can* (San Bernardino: Here's Life, 1982), p. 166.

The following chapters expose myths that could destroy us. I pray it is not too late to arm ourselves with truth so that we can maintain the freedoms we enjoy. We are not shadow boxing—the battle is real and cannot be wished away.

2

THE MYTH THAT
LIFE BEGAN WITH
BLIND CHANCE

In British Columbia, five hundred miles northeast of Vancouver, the Fraser River parts into two streams— one runs east to the Atlantic Ocean, the other west to the Pacific. Once the water has parted, its direction is unchangeably fixed. The fork in the river is known as the Great Divide.

In our society there are critical issues that divide us as a nation. The side we take will influence the moral direction of America. Neutrality is not possible. We are all a part of the stream of ideas and must make our choice at the great divide.

The evolution/creation controversy is just such a juncture. It has far greater implications than the technical question of whether creation-science can properly be called "science." At stake is the more serious problem of whether we have a foundation for morality and meaning in the world or whether we must accept chaos and despair as a way of life.

Consider: If man is only a biological accident that arose by chance chemical reactions of impersonal forces, it is difficult if not impossible to make any distinction between right and wrong (the reasons for this will be given in the next chapter). But if a Creator is responsible for the universe and man's place in it, then moral behavior and the search for meaning can quite possibly lead to a satisfying conclusion.

Secular humanism is in a catch-twenty-two situation. On the one hand it professes an interest in building a more humane world and glorifies man as the supreme ruler in the universe. But when this noble view of man is combined with atheism, a problem immediately arises. Where did man come from? The humanist must resort to the theory of evolution to explain man's origin. There he discovers that man descended from the lower animals and differs from them only qualitatively, not in kind. In other words, he is more intelligent than other animals but does share their nature and origin.

Consequently, the honored place given to man is quickly aborted by the grim realization that he is but an animal trying to find his way in a world where there are no values. With one hand the humanist exalts man; with the other he must drag him down to the level of camels and stones. B. F. Skinner, who saw the implications of an evolutionary-atheistic world view, asserted that man has neither the freedom nor the dignity that he once thought he possessed. In an atheistic world, man's uniqueness disappears. In his place is an animal subject to the same impersonal laws as dogs, apes, and worms.

Some scholars have tried to combine a belief in God with evolution, contending that God started the process and set up the laws that then took over. This view, known as theistic evolution, is inconsistent. After all, if evolution can do what it claims, God is unnecessary. And if God is needed at the beginning of the process, then it is just as easy to let Him be responsible for the initial creation and the species as we essential-

ly know them today. The crucial debate is atheistic
evolution versus the creative power of a personal
God. That, as we shall see, is the great divide.

Today the doctrine of evolution is in disarray. Although the man on the street may not know it yet, the
theory of evolution is being dismantled through modern discoveries. Dr. Paul LeMoine, a French scholar
and editor of *L'Encyclopedie Francais*, is quoted as
saying candidly, "Evolution is a fairy tale for adults."
Some of the reasons it can be shown to be a myth are
given below.

PROBLEMS WITH THE THEORY OF EVOLUTION

DARWINISM

Mention the word *evolution* and the name Charles
Darwin comes immediately to mind. He is rightfully
thought of as the Father of Evolution, even though
others such as Jean-Baptiste Lamarck propounded
similar theories before him. In his book *The Origin of
Species* Darwin says that after all of his research he
concluded that the view that each species has been
independently created is erroneous. How then did the
various species come about?

> As many more individuals of each species are born
> than can possibly survive; and as, consequently, there
> is a frequently reoccurring struggle for existence, it fol-
> lows that any being, if it vary however slightly in a
> manner profitable to itself, under the complex and
> sometimes varying conditions of life, will have a better
> chance of surviving and thus be *naturally selected*.
> From the strong principles of inheritance, any selected
> variety will tend to propagate its new and modified
> form.[1]

1. Charles Darwin, *Origin of Species* (Chicago: Thompson & Thomas,
n.d.), p. 457.

But how did life itself get started? In his early writings Darwin often referred to a Creator as the one responsible for the formation of a limited number of original forms of life. But by 1871, he began to speculate about the possibility of spontaneous generation to be the means by which life arose. He wrote,

> We could conceive in some warm little pond, with all sorts of ammonia and phosphoric salts, light, heat and electricity, etc. that a protein compound was chemically formed ready to undergo still more complex changes.[2]

Darwin's theory held that (1) life itself probably began by a chance combination of various existent chemicals, (2) subsequent changes were gradual, and (3) natural selection accounted for those that survived.

But Darwinism has fallen on hard times. Though natural selection might account for minor adaptations, it simply cannot explain the major differences among species. Consider the change from fish to air-breathing, four-legged animals—if the change had been gradual, whole generations would have perished during the transition. None would have survived.

Or think of the complex nipple used by the female whale for suckling its young under water without drowning the young one. As A. E. Wilder-Smith points out, no half-way stage of development from an ordinary nipple to the specialized nipple used for underwater feeding would be possible. All suckling whales would have drowned during the gradual development over thousands of years.

Gordon Rattray Taylor, himself an evolutionist, has written a penetrating critique of Darwinism in his

2. Francis Darwin, *The Life and Letters of Charles Darwin* (New York: Appleton, 1898), 2:202.

book *The Great Evolution Mystery.* Taylor points out
with scores of examples that Darwinism simply cannot
account for the radical changes we see today. Speaking of the eye he writes:

> It is harder, I think, to see how major structures like the
> eyelid appeared, for a small flap of skin would offer
> little advantage. Until an eyelid covers the eye, it is not
> much use. But what is really hard to swallow is the
> structure of the eye itself.
>
> As far as I know, no one has estimated the number of
> mutations which would be necessary to bring about all
> these changes, and not only changes but the creation
> of new structures (such as the iris) for which there was
> no precedent. Yet the essential features of the eye appeared quite abruptly in evolutionary terms. As we
> shall see later, this is not really long enough, bearing in
> mind that many mutations would do more harm than
> good. Moreover, the more complex the structure gets,
> the more precisely engineered must be any addition to
> it. In the end, it is a question of chance, and all depends
> on whether you think such an amazing sequence of
> lucky turns is credible or not.[3]

The fossil record also disproves Darwin's basic theory. Experts tell us that the fossils appear suddenly and
full-blown. An evolutionist, speaking in Chicago in
1982, admitted candidly that it is a trade secret that
missing links do not exist. If Darwinism were true,
there would be thousands of transitional forms. What
is truly remarkable is that most fossils are much like
the animals that exist today.

Somewhere I read that if you are going to jump
across a chasm it is much better to do it in one long
jump than in several short ones! Darwin attempted to

3. Gordon Rattray Taylor, *The Great Evolution Mystery* (New York: Harper
& Row, 1983), pp. 101-2.

do in a series of gradual changes what can be done only in one long jump. The gaps simply do not allow for gradual changes.

NEO-DARWINISM

To account for the radical changes in species, evolutionists were forced to conclude that variations arose suddenly, regardless of environmental conditions. Known as mutations, these special variations supposedly account for the gaps between species. To illustrate: Alligators laid eggs for thousands of years and hatched baby alligators. However one day, the theory goes, the egg hatched baby birds.

Of course such mutations are contrary to what scientists observe in nature today. But remember, for the atheist, evolutionists *must* be right. The fact that almost all mutations that take place are harmful, and in no instance has one ever produced a form of life having both greater complexity and greater viability than its ancestors, is dismissed.

Today scientists frequently suggest other ways that the gaps might be bridged. It is fashionable to speak of "directed chance" or "biochemical predestination." Thus the variations were not due so much to chance but to the "striving" or "purposiveness" of some kind of Life Force that is unknown today. Of course, some scientists stoutly resist this explanation of origins because of its implications. Gordon Rattray Taylor himself is forced to speak of some directive influence in evolution but writes, "While some scientists have felt forced to postulate some directive influence in evolution, others froth at the mouth at the mere idea. This is because they fear that we shall revert to believing in a divine plan."[4]

4. Ibid., pp. 5-6.

Taylor himself accepts such a directive force but does not want to resort to God. But what is such "purposiveness in nature" if not the hint of a divine mind? C. S. Lewis, speaking about such a view, correctly observed, "The Life-Force is a sort of tame god. You can switch it on when you want, but it will not bother you. All the thrills of religion and none of the cost. Is the Life-Force the greatest achievement of wishful thinking the world has yet seen?"[5]

The obstacles against believing that life began by the forces of blind chance are formidable. Atheistic evolution requires a degree of faith that can be achieved only by those who are determined to believe regardless of the odds.

THE SPECIAL CONDITIONS NEEDED FOR LIFE

If life began by a "fortuitous concourse of atoms," what conditions would be needed for this stroke of luck? In 1934 a Russian scientist, Aleksandr Oparin, published a book suggesting that lightning and ultraviolet light might have synthesized biologically when life began in the primitive ocean.

In 1954 experiments were conducted in the United States by Stan Miller, whose synthesis in a laboratory produced sizable quantities of amino acids and other organic molecules. Later adenine, one of the components of DNA, was synthesized from a mixture of ammonia, methane, and water. Thus the building blocks of life were brought about through human experimentation.

But even with the synthesis of amino acids in a highly controlled laboratory, scientists agree that life cannot be sustained without protein, and proteins come only from life. In other words, life would already have to have been here before it began. As evolutionist

5. C. S. Lewis, *Mere Christianity* (New York: Macmillan, 1952), p. 35.

Taylor admits, "The fundamental objection to all these theories is that they involve raising oneself by one's own bootstraps. You cannot make proteins without DNA, but you cannot make DNA without enzymes which are proteins. It is a chicken and egg situation."[6] Creationist A. E. Wilder-Smith uses this example: If a baby suddenly appeared without a mother, it would die. Hence even if a cell were to begin by random forces, it would immediately die because there would be no cradle for it.

Louis Pasteur, the noted nineteenth-century scientist, proved conclusively that spontaneous generation cannot arise from organic material. The evolutionist wants to assert that it arose from *inorganic* material—from the original chemicals in Darwin's "warm pond." The only explanation scientists have is the assumption that the laws of chemistry and physics must have been different when the earth was formed. There is no evidence for this, of course; it's just that atheists are convinced that evolution *has* to be right. After all, the only alternative is belief in God.

At any rate, scientists today, though having synthesized amino acids, have not been able to form a single cell that would duplicate itself. No scientist has ever advanced a testable procedure whereby the fantastic jump to complexity could have occurred, even if the universe had been filled with proteins. Once again Taylor admits, "Unless there was some inner necessity, some built-in primordial disposition to consolidate into such a pattern, it is past belief that anything so intricate and idiosyncratic should appear."[7]

Are we really to believe that what scientists cannot do in a controlled laboratory happened all by itself without the benefit of protein?

6. Taylor, p. 201.
7. Ibid., p. 207.

THE LAW OF RANDOMNESS

Living cells are exceedingly complex. To believe that the original molecules moved from randomness to complexity is contrary to everything we know about natural law. An evolutionist must believe that nonliving atoms slowly organized themselves into complex, energy-rich forms. But this is contrary to the law of enthropy, that is, that nature left to itself tends toward disorganization, not complexity.

Scientist Wilder-Smith gives this example: If you were to take a small aircraft, fly it 6,000 feet over your home, and throw out 100,000 white cards, which had been neatly stacked in the plane, what is the possibility of their landing to form your initials? Obviously the chances are nil. Throwing them out of the plane would cause them to have more disorganization than when they were stacked in a neat pile.

Evolutionists usually counter this argument by suggesting that within time anything can happen. If the earth is several billion years old, the basic principle of nature might just happen to have been reversed. But as Wilder-Smith suggests, let us assume that with the help of tiny parachutes we could give each card a much longer time to flutter down to the earth—let's say twenty years. Does this increase the possibility that the cards will neatly be arranged to form your initials? Of course not. The greater the time, the greater the randomness.

Or consider putting various bits of metal into a barrel and shaking it for a million years. What are the chances of forming a wristwatch? And if the millions of years turned out to be billions, would your chance be greater?

The important point to be made in these illustrations is that a single cell has much more complexity than the initials of your name or even a wristwatch. Since the unraveling of the DNA code, we have a better appreciation for what is needed to create a human being. Each person has approximately 30 trillion cells in his body. Each cell contains 46 chromosomes (23 from each parent). The activity within a single cell is equivalent to that of a large city such as Tokyo or Chicago. Each cell has genetic information that programs it to become a part of one of the many different parts of the body. Walter T. Brown writes, "The genetic information contained in each cell of the human body is roughly equivalent to a library of 4,000 volumes."[8] If we multiply that by 30 trillion, we can begin to appreciate the complexity of a single human being. Donald M. Mackay, a specialist in brain research, describes the complexity of the brain this way:

> In order to form a realistic idea of the structural complexity inside your head, imagine that one cubic millimeter of your cerebral cortex were magnified to the size of a lecture hall. In this magnified one millimeter cube we might expect to find something of the order of 100,000 nerve cells. If each of these had 1,000 to 10,000 connections, each connection adjustable in ways that might be functionally important, then within this one hall we would have a tangled structure containing up to a *thousand million* functionally significant elements. Depicted on the same scale, the nerve fibers running from the brain to other parts of your body would extend for distances up to a thousand kilometers.

> Now let us take the arithmetic a step farther. The human cortex is about 2,000 square centimeters in area, and on average about three millimeters thick. In order to complete our imaginary model of your brain on the same scale, then, we would need something like 600,000 of these lecture halls stacked side by side and three deep. That is the kind of complexity that chal-

8. Walter T. Brown, *In the Beginning* (Naperville, Ill.: I.C. R. Midwest Center, 1981), p. 3.

lenges the scientist as he contemplates your brain, ticking peacefully away inside your head as you sit in your chair.[9]

To assume that all of this was put together by chance is beyond belief. In the creation-science trial in Arkansas in December 1981, observers were surprised to find two distinguished scientists who themselves had been evolutionists. One was Chandra Wickramasinghe, an astrophysicist in Wales, and the other was Sir Fred Hoyle. These men now believe that the existence of a creator can be established by mathematics with a probability greater than 1 to 10 with 40,000 zeros. Hoyle reported that the chances of forming a typical cell by randomly combining imino acids are about the same as the chance of solving Rubic's Cube by haphazard twists. Their conclusions are shared by other scientists who have established the same kind of probability ratios. The late H. Quastler calculated the odds as 1 in 10 with 301 zeros. Remember that, even with such a stroke of luck, we must still believe that this individual cell reproduced and eventually led to the complexity of life as we know it today. Mathematically such a probability is equivalent to believing that there was an explosion in a print factory and the result was a Webster's Dictionary.

Scientists have been so baffled with how life could begin that Francis Crick and Leslie Orgel, once at Cambridge University but now at the Salk Institute in California, have toyed with the possibility that life was deliberately transmitted to chosen planets by an advanced civilization somewhere else in the universe. A more recent writer, William R. Fix, author of *The Bone*

9. Donald M. Mackay, *Brains, Machines and Persons* (Grand Rapids: Eerdmans, 1980), pp. 23-24.

Peddlers: The Selling of Evolution, has suggested that the earth is populated with spirits who began life somewhere in the distant past.

Of course, these theories only cast the shadow of evolution further back. They do not give a scientific explanation of how life began but punt the ball to an *ad hoc* hypothesis. It's the last desperate attempt of man to try to explain the universe without God.

THE EXISTENCE OF THE UNIVERSE

That God created the universe *ex-nihilo* is rejected by evolutionary scientists as unscientific because it involves supernatural action. Thus, creationism can no longer be taught in the public schools of America.

Yet, incredibly, some evolutionists maintain that the universe itself *evolved out of nothing.* Even though this would contradict known laws of cause and effect, such a belief has been postulated by men such as Edward P. Tryon, professor of physics at the City University of New York. He said, "In 1973, I proposed that our universe had been created spontaneously from nothing (ex-nihilo) as a result of established principles of physics. This proposal variously struck people as preposterous, enchanting, or both."[10]

Admittedly, it does strike one as preposterous, yet today many evolutionists are taking it seriously. Allen Guth has promoted the concept of an "inflationary universe." He says that at the beginning the entire universe of space, time, and matter was concentrated as an infinitesimal particle with all force systems (gravity, electromagnetic, nuclear, and weak forces) unified as a single type of force. This entity somehow inflated at a rapid rate, and the various forces be-

10. Edward P. Tryon, "What Made the World?" *New Scientist* 101 (8 March 1984):14.

came separated. In commenting on this novel theory Tryon says, "In this scenario, the 'hot big bang' was preceded by the 'cold big swoosh.' "[11]

Dozens of questions remain unanswered, including, Where did the original energy and matter come from? What caused this explosion? How could impersonal forces acting randomly construct a universe whose planets rotate with such precision that we set our clocks by them? That the sun just happened to be the right distance from the earth, and that the dozens of other conditions needed for life arose blindly, staggers the imagination. Creationists simply do not have enough faith for evolution. It is preposterous to believe that *nothing times nobody equals everything.*

Is Creationism Scientific?

Today the evolution/creation controversy is haughtily debated. Should creationism be taught in public schools, or would that be teaching religion? In 1981 a trial was held in Arkansas to determine whether creationism should be taught along with evolution as an alternate approach to the question of origins. The American Civil Liberties Union (ACLU) spent $2 million to prepare its case against the "balanced treatment act," which would necessitate teaching both models of origins in our schools. The evolutionists won; the creationists lost.

The ACLU argued that creationism is not a science but primarily a biblical concept. Hence, to teach creationism is to teach religion in the schools.

What is more, scientists do not like to accept supernatural explanations for any aspect of scientific experiment. They point out that years ago a solar eclipse was attributed to gods but now we know it to

11. Ibid., p. 3.

be a natural phenomenon. The hope is that someday the mystery of origins will likewise be explained.

Neither do scientists like to reckon with the unpredictability of God. Science wants to discover natural laws that can be used to produce future activity, but God is beyond telescopes and experiments. The existence of such a Being does not fit into the scientific "box."

Of course, neither the evolutionist nor the creationist can verify how the universe came into being. No one was there when it all began; we can produce neither the big bang nor the act of creation in the laboratory. Both views, therefore, are faith commitments.

But scientists develop models or "working hypotheses" of what they think happened. Experiments and study either tend to confirm or disprove the plausibility of these theories. Since the available evidence suggests that life began suddenly, and the possibility of life's beginning with blind chance is for all practical purposes zero, it stands to reason that creationism should be considered as a possible solution to the problem of origins. Creationism certainly takes less faith than the fairy tale for adults.

But isn't this teaching religion? Norman Geisler, who defended creationism at the Arkansas trial, pointed out correctly, "If teaching a part of a religion is automatically teaching that religion, then teaching values (such as freedom and tolerance) is also teaching religion. But the courts have ruled that values can be taught apart from religion, which may hold the same values. Likewise, creationism can be taught apart from the religious systems of which they may be a part."[12]

There is another good reason both models should

12. Norman L. Geisler, "Creationism: A Case for Equal Time," *Christianity Today,* 19 March 1982, p. 29.

be taught in our schools. The famous ACLU lawyer Clarence Darrow argued in the 1925 Scopes Trial that it is "bigotry for public schools to teach only one theory of origins." Today, of course, the ACLU is not open to such pluralism but insists that only one theory of origins be taught. Bigotry has returned to the public school classroom.

THE EVOLUTIONIST AND GOD

Behind the evolution/creation controversy is modern man's well-known aversion toward belief in God. To him any theory, preposterous as it may be, is more gladly accepted than belief in a Creator. That life was seeded here by other planetary beings, or by spirits that roamed primeval oceans, it is more inviting than to believe that a personal God exists. As D. M. S. Watson, an evolutionist, candidly admits, it is "a theory universally accepted not because it can be proven by logically coherent evidence to be true, but because the only alternative, special creation, is clearly incredible."[13]

Julian Huxley was once on a television program in which he responded to the question of why evolution was so readily accepted. He admitted, "The reason we accepted Darwinism even without proof, is because we didn't want God to interfere with our sexual mores." The real reason modern man does not want to believe in God is that he wants no interference from the Creator.

Evolutionist Gordon Taylor confesses freely that modern scientists have many doubts about evolution. But he adds, "It is unfortunate that the creationists are exploiting this new atmosphere by pressing their posi-

13. D. M. S. Watson, *Nature* (1929), quoted in Duane T. Gish, *Evolution? The Fossils Say No!* (San Diego: Creation Life, 1973), p. 24.

tion; this naturally drives the biologists into defensive attitudes and discourages them from making any admissions."[14] Thus many scientists secretly must admit that the evidence for the fairy tale is crumbling. However, they refuse to run toward God but insist in running away from Him. "There is none who understands, there is none who seeks for God" (Romans 3:11). If you do not wish to find God you will not, regardless of the evidence.

As we shall see in the next chapter, an evolutionary view of man leads to frightening conclusions. As a nation, we must make our choice at the Great Divide and then live with the consequences. To change the figure of speech, once we have bought our ticket, we must follow the train to its destination. We shall shortly learn that the evolutionary train terminates at meaninglessness, despair, and the abolition of decency and morality.

14. Taylor, p. 245.

3

THE MYTH THAT
WE CAN HAVE MORALITY
WITHOUT RELIGION

On November 17, 1980, the Supreme Court struck down a Kentucky law that required the posting of the Ten Commandments in public school classrooms. The justices ruled that having them before the students was a form of state-sponsored religious indoctrination prohibited by the first amendment. The Court said that the Ten Commandments were "plainly religious . . . and may induce children to read, meditate upon, perhaps to venerate and to obey the commandments."[1]

The basis of the Court's decision was the first amendment, "Congress shall make no law respecting the establishment of religion, or prohibiting the free exercise thereof." Some contemporary lawmakers interpret this phrase to mean that religious values should have no part in education, government, or society in general. Though its intention was to limit state control,

1. John Whitehead, *The Second American Revolution* (Elgin, Ill.: David C. Cook, 1982), pp. 109-10.

it is being reinterpreted today to mean the restriction of religious influence.

This new understanding of the separation between religion and politics is often used as an excuse to hold secular values in public life. The 1984 Democratic Vice-Presidential candidate Geraldine Ferraro stated that although she personally is opposed to abortion, she supports a woman's right to choose, because Mrs. Ferraro wants to "keep religion out of politics." The implication is that abortion is a religious issue and therefore should play no part in a political campaign.

But can morality and religion be separated? Admittedly the Ten Commandments are religious, but they are also a moral document. When the Supreme Court made its decision to have the commandments removed, one of the most succinct and clear moral codes available was taken from the walls of classrooms. As for abortion, Mrs. Ferraro was right that abortion is a religious issue, but *it is also a moral issue.* No one can sidestep the matter on the grounds that it is religious and not political.

The humanists make the most of word games. When a minister preaches against abortion, he is told that he should stay out of politics; when a politician wants to neutralize the abortion issue, he can insist that he wants to keep religion out of politics. One day it is only a political issue; the next it is religious.

Morality and religion can never be divorced. In fact, the basis of morality is the existence of God. Morality and religion are Siamese twins that cannot be separated. If they are, morality will die. "But," someone objects, "that's not true! You can stamp out religion from our schools and government and still have morality, because morality can exist independently of religion." Plausible though this may seem, careful scrutiny will show that it is impossible. Admittedly, nonreligious people have morality, but as we shall see they do so at the price of living inconsistently with what they profess to believe. Though they deny God, they nevertheless live *as if* they were created by Him.

Let me say with clarity: *God is absolutely necessary for morality.* No moral theory can arise out of atheism. Those who wish to create a secular state where religion has no influence will of necessity bring about meaninglessness, lawlessness, and despair. Such conditions often spawn a totalitarian state, instituted to restore order by brute force. When a nation loses its moral roots, a dictator often arises who takes away personal freedoms to restore order. In his own perverse way, a dictator also indirectly affirms the existence of God. But because his atheism does not allow him to give his subjects dignity, he can justify his brutality.

Morality is a child of religion; if, like the prodigal, it leaves home without its parents, it will end in the swamp of moral bankruptcy. To think that we can have morality without God is like believing that you can have trees without roots, petals without flowers.

In no past era has a culture been able to maintain morality and political freedom without the support of religious values. The atheist David Hume argued that even murder is not a vice but simply an act that excites passions within us.[2] But what if society actually accepted Hume's conclusions? Morality, which is the building block of society, would disappear.

Humanists themselves admit they are attempting a difficult task in trying to erect morality without religion. In the February 1977 issue of *Humanist* magazine Will Durant said, "Moreover, we shall find it no easy task to mold a natural ethic strong enough to maintain moral restraint and social order without the

2. David Hume, *A Treatise of Human Nature* (Oxford: Clarendon, 1888), p. 468.

support of supernatural consolations, hopes, and fears."[3] He continues, "There is no significant example in history, before our time, of a society successfully maintaining moral life without the aid of religion."[4]

Durant has underestimated the problem. It is not merely *difficult* to have morality without religion, it is *impossible*.

REASONS THAT MAN CANNOT BUILD A MORAL ETHIC WITHOUT GOD

THE LIMITS OF HUMAN WISDOM

One of the most startling statements made in the Bible is Paul's remark, "Has not God made foolish the wisdom of the world?" (1 Corinthians 1:20). This statement seems to contradict the great advances in science that we have witnessed in this generation. Man is able to go to the moon and return safely; he can build computers that do complex mathematical problems in split seconds; he can perform a triple bypass operation on the human heart. And yet, God says, the wisdom of man is foolishness. Does not science appear to conflict with this dismal evaluation of human wisdom?

The discrepancy can be easily resolved. As long as man explores the physical creation he is able to discover laws that he can creatively use in scientific experiments. God has given this world almost unlimited resources, and man is learning how to use the creation. The discovery of electricity makes it possible for us to light the cities of this nation; millions of tons of steel can be manufactured from the earth's resources for cars and airplanes.

But when man begins to speculate on that which is

3. Will Durant, *The Humanist*, February 1977, p. 26.
4. Ibid.

nonempirical—that which lies beyond the senses—he gropes for understanding. Knowledge of this world does not help him in metaphysical speculations in religion and ethics. Science can teach us how to make a hydrogen bomb but can give us no guidance as to when the bomb should be used. Science is silent regarding values. Therefore the truly important matters, the ultimate questions of the purpose of man's existence and his relationship to God, cannot be discovered by human reasoning. For that we need special revelation.

Why is man unable to erect a moral system from an atheistic viewpoint? First, he can never move from what *is* to what *ought to be.* He can study various cultures, but he cannot take the next step and say what *ought* to be done. He can find no measuring stick by which diverse cultures can be judged. He can collect facts but cannot prescribe actions.

David Hume was the first to articulate this dilemma. He concluded that it is impossible to say that any action is morally wrong. As already noted, he believed that actions such as murder and stealing are not wrong but simply elicit negative feelings. Morality is nothing but a matter of personal preference.

Jacques Monod, a French molecular biologist, in an interview in the *New York Times* agreed that it is impossible to derive what ought to be from what is. He said that if there was no intention in the universe, and if we are pure accidents of evolution, then we cannot discover what ought to be. He concluded that values must be chosen arbitrarily, without any standard by which to judge them.

The Judeo-Christian viewpoint overcomes this dilemma. God determines what ought to be. Although man is not able to construct a moral standard, the Creator is. Morality becomes possible.

A second reason man cannot develop a moral

code on his own is because he lacks the needed perspective. All we have at our disposal is bits and pieces of experience. We are like a mole who encounters this clump of dirt and that blade of grass, but is unable to see the whole picture. William James once remarked that we are like dogs in a library seeing the volumes but unable to read the print—an apt description of man's dilemma if he is alone in the universe.

Is it possible on a humanistic basis to conclude that lying is wrong? No, because atheism cannot own such an objective standard. The humanist cannot say that lying is wrong because it leads to bad results. Often lying has led to beneficial results—at least in the present world. We recall the words of the Sunday school boy, "Lying is an abomination unto the Lord but a very present help in time of trouble." Sometimes it is dishonesty and not honesty that pays.

Left to himself, man cannot distinguish right from wrong. Though he has acquired great knowledge of the physical world, he is ignorant regarding the invisible world of religion and values.

Ludwig Wittgenstein, who influenced the direction of analytical philosophy, candidly admitted in the *Philosophical Review* that if there are ethical absolutes, they would have to come to man from *outside* of the human situation. He writes, "If a man could write a book on ethics which really was a book on ethics, this book would, with an explosion destroy all the other books in the world."[5] Then he adds "Ethics, if it is anything, is supernatural and our words will express only facts."[6] Wittgenstein did not believe that such a supernatural revelation existed; but he saw clearly that if there was no such help from a supernatural source,

5. Ludwig Wittgenstein, "Wittgenstein's Lectures on Ethics," *Philosophical Review* 74 (1965):7.
6. Ibid.

all of man's talk about good and evil is nonsense. At best, man can describe facts, but ethical statements are all on the same plane. "My conscience tells me to burn a widow with the corpse of her husband," a pagan told a British officer. The officer replied, "My conscience tells me to hang you if you do." Without an objective standard from outside the human situation, morality is simply a matter of personal feeling.

THE QUEST FOR MEANING

Some time ago I read of a New York police officer who saw a man standing on a bridge, apparently contemplating suicide. The officer went to him and said, "Let me make a deal with you. Give me ten minutes to tell you why I think life is worth living, then you take ten minutes and tell me why you think life is not worth living. If I am unable to convince you, I will let you jump." The story goes that twenty minutes later they joined hands and both of them jumped into the water!

Can there be meaning in a world without God? Albert Camus, in the first sentence of *The Myth of Sisyphus* wrote, "There is but one truly serious philosophical problem, and that is suicide." He understood clearly that if his atheism is to be consistently applied, man cannot find values in the world.

Actually the situation is even more serious than Camus thought. It's not just that values elude man in an atheistic world, but more accurately he cannot even logically speak of them.

Why?

Remember the evolutionary view of man is that life began somewhere in Darwin's "warm pond." The atoms randomly assembled themselves into a complex pattern, and suddenly a living cell appeared. This cell began to reproduce itself, and hence the whole chain of being got started. All life is therefore derived from chemical compounds plus energy. Man, like the animals from which he evolved, is composed solely of matter. He has no spirit, no soul, but is simply a physical organism. As the French philosopher Julien Offray de LaMettrie put it, "Let us conclude boldly then, that man is a machine, and that in the whole universe there is but a single substance with various modifications."[7] He accepted the implications of a mechanistic theory of origin and affirmed that all human actions were predetermined by chemistry and physics. Freedom, in any sense of the word, is an illusion.

In the nineteenth century, Thomas Huxley embraced a similar form of reductionism. He believed that just as the noise of a babbling brook is only a by-product of the rushing water, so the mind is simply a by-product of the brain. But just as the babbling cannot influence the brook, so the mind cannot influence the brain. He maintained that mind is an "epiphenomenon" of matter, that is, an attendant or secondary phenomenon, a spontaneous by-product of the interplay of matter in motion. He believed that thoughts are but the expression of molecular changes.

Consider the implications: the evolutionist does not believe in the existence of the soul or mind since a spiritual substance cannot arise out of evolving matter. What we call the mind is just the product of physical and chemical changes in the brain. *Therefore evolutionists believe that matter can think.*

But if matter can think, we have a difficulty: Since we don't control physical and chemical laws that control matter, we have no control whatever over our thoughts. What I think depends on the chemical reactions of the calcium and phosphate in my brain.

7. Julien Offray de LaMettrie, *Man a Machine* (1747), in Norman L. Torrey, ed., *Les Philosophes* (New York: Capricorn, 1960), p. 177.

Therefore it follows that if evolution is correct, humans have no responsibility for their actions. Since we can't say that one combination of chemical reactions is more ethical than another, all thoughts are morally neutral. Whatever *is, is.* Morality does not exist.

Reread the last paragraph if you have to. Evolutionists are caught in a dilemma. If ideas are reduced to special combinations of atoms (as is necessary in an evolutionary world view), and since those atoms are out of my control, my thoughts are predetermined by natural law. Obviously I am not a moral being.

What is the alternative? The Bible teaches that in addition to man's brain, he also possesses a soul or mind that is not bound by natural law. That's why we can hold a man accountable for murder and child abuse. But if he has only a brain, he has no more control over his thoughts than he does the composition of his gastric juices. Another materialist, Pierre Cabanis, wrote, "The brain secretes thought as the liver secretes bile." We don't control the quality of our bile, therefore we can't control our thoughts either— they are determined for us by the laws of physics and chemistry.

Many attempts have been made by humanists to escape the unwelcome conclusion that if there is no God and man evolved from matter, he cannot be a responsible being. Whether it is Julian Huxley's epiphenomenon or Thomas Hobbes's materialism, the fact is that there can be no morality in a world where all reality is but a collection of atoms.

If you have followed the argument this far, you can see that if we have been thrown up by the haphazard forces of nature, we cannot even trust our ability to reason. Charles Darwin himself once said, "The horrid doubt always arises whether the convictions of a man's mind, which has developed from the mind of lower animals, are of any value or at all trust-worthy. Would anyone trust the conviction of a monkey's mind, if there are any convictions in such a mind?"[8] In other words, even if Darwinism is true, there is no way of establishing its plausibility. In a chance universe, logic must be ruled out.

But someone may object: "Can't the humanist argue for morality simply on the basis that we should do whatever is best for the human race?" Such a question already presupposes a religious understanding of man's origin. If man is the product of the happenstance of evolution, if he is only atoms and his thoughts are only chemical reactions, the words *best* and *value* simply do not apply. To thus use them is to misuse language. It's like someone saying that the choir music sounded red or that a tree has a charming personality. Remember, the conclusion of humanism must be that whatever *is*, just *is*. Nothing more can be said.

Jean-Paul Sartre understood clearly where atheism led. "All activities are equivalent . . . thus it amounts to the same thing whether one gets drunk alone or is a leader of nations."[9] It is not just a matter of having an inadequate morality or a wrong morality, but it is a matter of morality's not existing at all.

Of course, as we shall see, humanists do talk about morality. But when they do, they piggyback on the Judeo-Christian ethic. When they believe in human dignity, freedom, and peace, they are assuming a theistic view of the world.

MAN'S SEARCH FOR VALUE

Where does all of this leave us? The atheist says we are one with the animal world. Strictly speaking, we

---

8. From a letter to W. Graham, 3 July 1881, quoted in Charles Darwin, *The Autobiography of Charles Darwin and Selected Letters* (1892; reprint ed., New York: Dover, 1958).
9. Jean-Paul Sartre, *Being and Nothingness,* trans. Hazel E. Barnes (New York: Washington Square, 1965), p. 627.

can no longer speak of you and me, because we are just "its." We've already learned that a being thrown up by chance and composed entirely of atoms can hardly be thought of as worthy.

Occasionally one finds atheists who are willing to admit the inescapable conclusion of their presuppositions. When all of the rhetoric finally ceases and the implications are acknowledged, atheists speak with clarity. For example, Oliver Wendell Holmes, a Supreme Court Justice from 1902 to 1932, said,

> I see no reason for attributing to man a significant difference in kind from that which belongs to a baboon or a grain of sand. I believe that our personality is a cosmic ganglion, just as when certain rays meet and cross there is white light at the meeting point.[10]

This of course is precisely where the atheistic-evolutionary view leads. This is humanism brought to its disappointing conclusion. Man may be more complex, but he has no more significance than a baboon or a grain of sand. Abortion, infanticide, and euthanasia all become possible in a world where human life is seen as the product of evolutionary forces.

Bertrand Russell, the famous British atheist, acknowledged that "man is the product of causes which had no provision of the end they were achieving; his origin, his growth, his hopes and fears, his loves and his beliefs are but the outcome of accidental collocations of atoms . . . blind to good and evil, reckless of destruction, omnipotent matter rolls on its relentless way."[11]

When the Supreme Court asked that the Ten Commandments be removed from Kentucky classrooms,

10. Quoted in Whitehead, p. 52.
11. Bertrand Russell, *Mysticism and Logic* (New York: Norton, 1929), pp. 47-48.

they had no moral code to replace them. Logically, all that would be left is a blank wall. When religion is removed, morality goes too.

WHY ARE ATHEISTS MORAL?

Picture a man sitting on the end of a horizontal steel bar. He is kept in balance by the weight of another man sitting on the opposite end. The bar itself is suspended from a rope fastened over the edge of a cliff. One man steadies himself enough to pull a gun from his vest pocket. He aims carefully and shoots the man at the other end. The obvious result: Both men fall into the chasm below.

When humanists attempt to destroy belief in God, they cannot do so without destroying themselves. They may champion human rights and speak of the need for morality, but their philosophy has no metaphysical basis to sustain such values.

We have seen that no values can arise from an atheistic world view. Yet the fact remains that many atheists are moral individuals, trustworthy and caring. How can this be?

The answer is that they were created in God's image and were given a moral consciousness just as all other human beings. This explains why they can speak about right and wrong, about tolerance and freedom. They do so not because they are able to justify the use of such terminology from an atheistic viewpoint but because the image of God exists in every man.

Hence, a man who pays his bill and speaks about love and yet affirms atheism is a living contradiction. He is like branches that deny the existence of the tree that bears them; he is like a fish swimming in the ocean, confidently asserting that no water exists in the universe.

An atheist's logic tells him that he is of no more value than a baboon or a grain of sand, yet his life contradicts such a conclusion. He may provide for his wife and family, and if you were to steal his car he would want you to be punished—all this because he is created in the image of God.

We have not yet seen the full result of humanism in the United States. We are still coasting on the values derived from our rich Judeo-Christian heritage. There was a time in American history when the Scriptures were widely regarded as authoritative in matters of religion and morals. Most people thought in terms of absolutes; some actions were invariably wrong, others were right. Puritanism, which today carries a stigma it does not fully deserve, had strict moral codes. Obviously there was not always unanimous agreement regarding moral issues, but the primary moral laws were accepted. But as religious liberalism began its attack on the Scriptures, and as philosophers rejected the doctrine of a personal God, man became depersonalized. Without a word from outside the universe, he was cast out on a sea without a shore. Secularism reminded him of the despair and futility that were to be his legacy.

The older generation has not yet fully felt this influence. They keep thinking of the good old days when moral codes were accepted, truth was upheld, and modesty was a virtue. But a good segment of the older population has also rejected the Scriptures as a revelation of a personal God. Therefore they have no basis for the values they inherited from the past. These people, as Francis Schaeffer states, simply function on a past memory.

What we all must understand is that if the Scriptures are not accepted, and man is left to define his own ethics, there is no reason any form of morality at all should be accepted. There is no reason for the older generation to ask, "What is this world coming to?" It is simply arriving at the destination made inevitable by the inroads of humanism in our educational system, government, and the media. The younger generation has tried to be consistent in its moral philosophy. If there is no God, no absolute, no meaning, why should the traditions of the past be accepted? Why anything?

Without a return to scriptural authority, the future can be predicted with some measure of accuracy. The generations that follow will probably be more consistent than the present generation, which has clung to some absolutes without any justification. Presumably such vestigial moral remains will be gone in the future. Humanism will be consistently applied. That which was formerly classified as good can then be considered evil, previous evil can be regarded as good, everyone will be permitted to do whatever seems right in his own eyes, and chaos will prevail.

If we wish to stop this moral toboggan slide we must once again proclaim the Scriptures as an authoritative revelation from a sovereign God who pronounces judgment on those who regard evil as good and good as evil (Isaiah 5:20). The biblical doctrines of sin, judgment, and salvation must once again be heard with clarity and power. As individuals come to trust Christ personally, the Holy Spirit will give them the power to live righteously. Second, we who know Christ must live lives that properly exemplify Christian conduct. Christianity is true even if no one lives the Christian life; but few people believe unless Christians themselves live lives beyond reproach.

Fortunately, a growing number of individuals of all ages are resisting the onslaught of humanistic values in our culture. Many, like the prophet Daniel, have determined not to defile themselves with the social values of their generation. Deep personal commitment is needed to withstand the pressures of our permissive society, and such commitment is not optional. If the choice is (as it appears to be) between a return to biblical morality or the acceptance of consistent humanism, the people of this nation must make a crucial decision—a decision that cannot be postponed indefinitely. We must either return to a biblically rooted moral ethic or learn to accept without rebuke legalism, rioting, bombings, stealing, murder, sexual perversion, and despair. If we want to return to biblical morality, it will be a long trip back. May God help us to take that first big step.

4

THE MYTH THAT
WHATEVER IS LEGAL
IS MORAL

After Hitler was defeated, war crime trials were held in Nuremberg to judge the guilt of Hitler's henchmen. But a dispute arose as to what laws should be used to try the accused. After all, Hitler's cronies argued—quite plausibly—they had not broken any laws; their actions were done within the protection of their own legal system. They could not be accused of murder, because personhood had been defined to exclude Jews and other minorities who were standing in the way of the advancement of the Third Reich. These men were simply following the laws made by the courts of the day. As Eichmann protested before his execution, "I had to obey the laws of war and my flag."

In our own country, a group of protesters who picketed an abortion clinic were charged with slander because they called abortionists murderers. The abortionists argued, just as Hitler's emissaries had done, that they could not be called murderers since they were not breaking any laws—you can't call someone who isn't breaking a law a murderer.

But the experience of Nuremberg and the silent holocaust perpetrated in our abortion clinics all bear eloquent witness to the fact that when a state believes it is accountable to no one except itself, it assumes a hidden premise, namely, whatever is legal is moral.

How shall we resolve a dispute between conflicting legal standards? Robert H. Jackson, chief counsel for the United States in the Nuremberg trials, was forced to appeal to permanent values, to moral standards transcending the life-styles of a particular society. In effect, he argued that there is "a law beyond the law" that stood in judgment on the arbitrary changing opinions of men.[1]

Whether or not such a law can be found will be discussed at the end of this chapter. For now, it is sufficient to remember that Hitler changed Germany by changing its laws. Today the shape of America is being altered by using the same strategy. America is, as John Whitehead has pointed out, being stolen. If the present trends continue, it will no longer be the land of the free; secular humanism will rewrite this country's laws and impose its ideology on us all. The Supreme Court has helped brainwash our people to believe that whatever is legal is moral. They would argue that there is no law above human laws. They would arrogantly agree with Georg W. F. Hegel that "the state is God walking on earth."

In order to understand how America is being stolen, let us trace the history of law in the United States.

EARLY LAW IN AMERICA

When the Pilgrims came to the United States they had some definite ideas about God, law, and politics.

---

1. Quoted in John Warwick Montgomery, The Law Above the Law (Minneapolis: Bethany House, 1975), pp. 25-26.

They came from England where freedom of worship
was severely restricted. Reacting against formality
and the strictures of the state church, they firmly intended to establish a country based upon principles
of freedom. But where could such principles be
found? They understood that belief in God was necessary if freedom were to survive. If the state were absolute, it would replace God as the supreme lawgiver.
When the Pilgrims signed the Mayflower Compact on
November 11, 1620, they pledged themselves in the
name of God and for the glory of God to advance the
Christian faith.

Later when the Declaration of Independence and
subsequently the Constitution were written, our founding fathers emphasized their faith in God. Deist Benja-
min Franklin gave what is now a famous acknowl-
edgment of God's sovereignty in the affairs of men.

> I have lived, sir, a long time, and the longer I live, the
> more convincing proof I see of this truth—that God gov-
> erns in the affairs of men. And if a sparrow cannot fall
> to the ground without His notice, is it probable that an
> empire can rise without His aid? We have been as-
> sured, sir, in the sacred writings, "that except the Lord
> build the house, they labor in vain that build it." I firmly
> believe this; and I also believe that without His concur-
> ring aid we shall succeed in this political building no
> better than the builders of Babel.

Today there is a debate as to how Christian the
founding fathers were. But whether they were individually Christian or not, there was a general consensus
of theism, the belief that God existed. And the new
republic was based upon this foundation.

This understanding profoundly affected their view
of law. Since man was responsible to his Creator, there
were absolute standards by which moral judgments
could be measured.

A theistic view of law was passed on to the American Colonies through Samuel Rutherford's book *Lex Rex*, or *The Law and the Prince*, written in 1644. This book was an attack against the divine right of kings; it insisted that even princes should be subject to the law.[2]

The eighteenth-century jurist William Blackstone also influenced early American understanding of law. He believed there were two sources of revelation, the Bible and nature. Since God is the personal omnipotent Creator, He works and governs in the affairs of men. Law should be consistent with His revelation in the Bible and nature (such as the relationship between parents and their children). No law should be passed that would be contrary to the law of God.

This understanding of law emphasized that (1) God is the source of all laws and (2) all men are created equal. Rutherford had reasoned that since all men are sinners, no man is superior to any other. This meant that even the king had to be subject to law— there were no exceptions. Notice how these two suppositions were embodied in the Declaration of Independence: "that all men are created equal, that they are endowed by their Creator with certain unalienable Rights."

These "unalienable" rights were considered as absolute rights that stemmed from man's creation by God. He did not have to prove his worthiness; his value was conferred upon him at creation. As a result, man is accountable to a higher authority other than men. All men must recognize that they are under the law of God.

This Christian view of the world so influenced the founding of this nation that in the words of C. Gregg

2. John W. Whitehead, *The Second American Revolution* (Elgin, Ill.: David C. Cook, 1982), p. 30.

Singer, it "so permeated the Colonial mind that it continued to guide even those who had come to regard the gospel with indifference or hostility. The currents of this orthodoxy were too strong to be easily set aside by those who in their own thinking had come to a different conception of religion and hence of government also."[3]

In years to come substantial changes would arise in the American understanding of law. With the erosion of a theistic base, law would no longer be based on an absolute view of morality; values would become relative and human worth devalued.

LAW IN TRANSITIONAL AMERICA

The strong influence of Christianity in law in America was weakened by several powerful influences.

First, there was evolution. Though Darwin continued to make references to the Creator, he later suggested that man might not have been created at all. Obviously if life had begun by a fortuitous combination of atoms in a distant "warm pond," man would have no obligation toward a deity.

But Darwinism was applied to other disciplines as well. Some argued that morals were constantly evolving and that ethics itself was based on "the survival of the fittest." This led to the belief that "might makes right."

Evolutionary theory was also applied to law. In 1870 Christopher Langdell, dean of Harvard School of Law, began to teach that the principles of evolution must be applied to the written opinion of judges. The conclusion was inescapable: Law was not what the constitution said it was, but what the judges said it was. In

3. C. Gregg Singer, A Theological Interpretation of American History, quoted in Whitehead, p. 34.

other words there was no longer an objective base; the absolutes dissolved along with the supposed demise of the Creator.[4]

The implications of this new understanding of law were later echoed by Justice Holmes when he said that laws are "beliefs that have triumphed and no more."[5] And again he said, "Truth is the majority vote of that nation that could lick all the others."[6] And again, "When it comes to a development of a *corpus juris* (or body of law) the ultimate question is what do the dominant forces of the community want and do they want it hard enough to disregard whatever inhibitions may stand in the way."[7] This evolutionary view of law eroded man's dignity and made the arbitrary taking of human life legally possible.

Second, Christianity was weakened by the introduction of liberal theology. The Bible was stripped of the miraculous and considered as one book among many. No longer was it generally believed that we have in our hands an objective revelation of God. In the end liberalism was reduced to humanism in theological dress.

All of these changes profoundly influenced the way law was understood. No longer was it true that man had certain "unalienable" rights derived from creation. Rather, he was free to make up his own laws as the situation dictated. John Warwick Montgomery summarizes how this sad state of affairs came about by pointing out that in the eighteenth century the Bible was killed by unwarranted destructive criticism; in the nineteenth century God was killed; and in our twentieth century inevitably man has been killed. Montgomery adds, "This degeneration is not acciden-

4. Whitehead, pp. 46-47.
5. Ibid., p. 50.
6. Ibid., p. 51.
7. Ibid.

tal; each step logically follows from what has preceded: The loss of the Bible leads to the loss of God, for in the Bible God is most clearly revealed; the loss of God leaves Man at the naked mercy of his fellows, where might makes right."[8]

A student of the history of law in the United States should have been able to predict that human life would soon be reclassified as unworthy of special protection. Abortion, infanticide, and euthanasia are the inevitable result of secular humanism's world view. When God dies, so does man.

LAW IN MODERN AMERICA

With the fading of the Christian world view, man now was king and able to make whatever laws he wanted. This has led to what Francis Schaeffer called "sociological law"—the belief that there are no absolutes but rather a relative, evolutionary morality. Law is what the majority wants or what the judges say it is. There is no higher court of appeal; no longer can one challenge a ruling on the basis of absolutes derived from a creator. Man, not God, is the source of laws.

As such, it is no longer possible to believe that all men were created equal. Since there was no creation, and we are but an evolving mass of chemicals, it was obvious that man would soon treat his fellows as animals treat their kin. Francis Crick, who won the Nobel Prize for his work in unraveling the DNA code, speaks for many when he says:

> You must realize that much of the political thinking of this country is very difficult to justify biologically. It was valid to say in the period of the American Revolution, when people were oppressed by priests and kings, that all men were created equal. But it doesn't have bio-

8. Montgomery, pp. 54-55.

logical validity. It may have some mystic validity in a religious context, but . . . it's not only biologically not true, it's also biologically undesirable. . . . We all know, I think, or are beginning to realize, that the future is in our hands, that we can, to some extent do what we want.[9]

Obviously Baby Doe, an infant who starved to death in Indiana because the parents refused to sign a treatment order, was hardly thought of as having been created equal. Because of his handicap he was considered unfit to live. He was not believed to be endowed by his Creator with certain unalienable rights. As we weed out weaker animals, so we now do with mankind. A court in New York ruled that the New York state legislature must determine which human beings are actually persons who are entitled to live.[10]

In 1973 the Supreme Court invalidated the abortion laws of fifty states and legalized, in effect, abortion on demand. Where did the Court get the notion that a woman has a right to an abortion? Since such a right is not found in the Constitution, the Court made it up. Remember, the Constitution is whatever the judges say it is. Thus the Court, like Napoleon, has crowned itself emperor and is answerable to no one except itself.

Although parental consent is needed for the prescribing of most medications, and especially for minor surgery, in 1976 the Court ruled that a girl under the age of eighteen has the right to have an abortion without parental consent. This exception was granted because the Court is intent on encouraging abortion

9. Quoted in John Whitehead, *The Stealing of America* (Westchester, Ill.: Crossway, 1983), p. 32.
10. Byrn v. New York City Health and Hospital Corp., 31 NY 2d. 194, 335 NYS 2d. 390, 393 (1972). Appeal dismissed 410 US 949 (1973).

for our nation's young people. And since it creates laws arbitrarily, it can make abortion an absolute right.

In some states young people under sixteen have the right to buy contraceptives without parental consent. If the parents do intervene, they could be prosecuted for standing in the way of a child's "rights." Certainly children have rights—the right to be loved, taught, and nourished. Also, the state has the right to interfere if a child is being abused. But if children's rights are enlarged, parental rights are proportionately diminished. There is an ominous tendency of the state to take away the parents' rights in favor of the children's rights. Thus, the state can interfere more readily in the life of the American family.

State rights, children's rights, and parental rights must be held in balance. Whenever anyone insists on his "rights," a right is usually taken away from someone else. The right of a woman to have an abortion takes away the right of a child to live; the right of children to live immorally takes away the right of parents to discipline them. This is consistent with life in a secular state where the children belong to the government, not to the parents. In communist countries the children are carefully educated by the state. Women are encouraged to work, assuring the fact that the children will not be trained at home. Only thus can the state be sure that its children will be "properly educated."

If the state has the right to take children away from parents who interfere with their child's freedom of expression, the influence of Christianity in our homes will be jeopardized. In all secular states Christianity is regarded as hindering self-expression. Hence, as the state encroaches on parent-child relationships, teaching Christianity to children could become illegal.

In 1963 the Supreme Court outlawed corporate

prayer in public school classrooms, and it is no longer constitutional to teach creationism alongside evolution. Academic interests can no longer be pursued in freedom. Teachers must teach the official state doctrine or else be dismissed for meddling in religion. Thus the right of every child to have a purely secular education is now promoted. Actually, the restrictions in our classrooms today resemble those in communist countries.

Jacques Ellul has pointed out that the whole point of learning in communist countries is to absorb the system's values. Chairman Mao of China, for example, simplified the script in his battle with illiteracy and thus was able to control what was being taught. The textbooks used to teach the adult students how to read, and which are the only ones to which they have access, are exclusively propaganda texts. Ellul states, "Thus, we see here a wonderful shaping tool. The illiterates are taught to read only the new script, nothing is published in that script except propaganda texts; therefore, the illiterates cannot possibly read— or know—anything else."[11]

Consider what Paul Blanshard wrote in the *Humanist* magazine under the title "Three Cheers for Our Secular State":

> I think that the most important factor moving us toward a secular society has been the educational factor. Our schools may not teach Johnny to read properly, but the fact that Johnny is in school until he is sixteen tends to lead toward the elimination of religious superstition. The average American child now acquires a high school education and this militates against Adam and Eve and all other myths of alleged history.[12]

11. Jacques Ellul, *Propaganda: The Formation of Men's Attitudes* (New York: Knopf, 1965), p. 110.
12. Paul Blanshard, "Three Cheers for Our Secular State," *Humanist* (March/April 1976): 17.

The secular state is never neutral but always uses propaganda to shape the attitudes and beliefs of its citizens. The humanists have a rather well-defined agenda that they want to impose upon those who attend our public schools.

And what about the church? A secular state will not operate according to the Constitution but will impose its own will upon the people to accomplish its goals of total secularization. Laws can be constructed to intentionally restrict religion to the sanctuaries of existing churches.

For example, in Los Angeles, participants in Bible studies were told to "cease and desist" because their homes were not zoned for church use. Fortunately, this law was later reversed, but it is a portent of things to come. By tightening restrictions for zoning laws, the ability of a church to build new facilities can be curtailed. And requiring permits for Bible studies will insure that the state is totally in control.

A few years ago the Supreme Court upheld the IRS ruling that denied tax exemption to Bob Jones University because the institution's racial stance was "contrary to public policy." But the racial controversy obscured the real issue, namely, freedom of religion. Many of us disagree with Bob Jones University's racial views but believe it has the right to hold such a belief on religious grounds. It is certainly feasible that churches that do not ordain women or homosexuals can have their tax-exempt status revoked because their beliefs are "contrary to public policy." Thus, under the guise of equality our religious freedoms can be taken away.

Pressure to bow to Caesar can be expected to escalate. Secularism will move inch by inch along its relentless way, smashing any opposition that it may encounter. Unless reversed, some form of totalitarianism with its disregard for human life and freedoms can be expected to emerge. Let us not think it can't happen here.

A BETTER WAY

As Christians we must explode the myth that whatever is legal is moral. We must point to "the law above the law" to be saved from arbitrary sociological laws. But we cannot do so by appealing to natural law or "the public interest." Such concepts remain vague and undefined, open to redefinition by each and every society. Communists for example by and large believe that massacre, labor camps, and the denial of due process of law are all within the "public interest." In 1971 my wife and I visited East Germany and toured Buchenwald, the site of one of Hitler's concentration camps. Engraved on the gates were the words "To each his own," implying that those who died there received the justice due them. As Montgomery points out, natural law "arrives at some notion of ultimacy, but its content is 'unknown.' "[13]

Jean Jacques Rousseau understood full well the need for an objective basis for law; but he also understood that such law could not be constructed by the finite knowledge of men. When discussing the role of the legislator he wrote:

> In order to discover the rules of society best suited to nations, a superior intelligence beholding all the passions of men without experiencing any of them would be needed. This intelligence would have to be wholly unrelated to our nature, while knowing it through and through; its happiness would have to be independent of us, and yet ready to occupy itself with ours; and lastly, it would have, in the march of time, to look forward to a distant glory, and, working in one century, to

13. Montgomery, p. 42.

be able to enjoy in the next. It would take gods to give men laws.[14]

Rousseau's request for a superior intelligence to give us laws actually exists. Through scriptural revelation God has given to us a higher law. John Montgomery lists several advantages that would be gained if we were to return to the Scriptures as a basis for law.[15] Three of these are summarized below:

(1) *A standard is provided by which men and societies can be evaluated and corrected.* Why should blacks and Jews receive equal protection under the law? Why were Nazi crimes of racism damnable? Not because of our current social values, which are subject to change, but because God has "made from one (blood) every nation of mankind to live on all the face of the earth" (Acts 17:26). And "there is neither Jew nor Greek, there is neither slave nor free man" (Galatians 3:28). Human equality is thus established on the rock of "higher law."

(2) *Scripture imparts gospel also; it contains not only the standard but also help for our fallen race.* Law not only has a political use—as the rule of society, but it also is, in Paul's words, "a tutor (schoolmaster) to lead us to Christ" (Galatians 3:24). Jesus in the Sermon on the Mount deepens its meaning, showing that sin goes beyond actions and originates in the human heart. Such revelation forces us to rely upon God's mercy and to receive the gift of forgiveness that is offered to all men everywhere.

(3) *Biblical revelation assures us of a last judgment where perfect justice shall be rendered.* Our le-

14. Ibid., pp. 36-37.
15. Ibid., pp. 45-57.

gal system suffers from the fallibility of the sinful human situation, but the Judge in the last day will at the same time be omniscient and just.

This belief in a "law above the law" means that the state is not absolute. *What men make legal is not necessarily moral.*

R. J. Rushdoony has observed that behind every system of law there is a god. "If the source of law is the individual, then the individual is the god of that system . . . if our source of law is our court, then the court is our god. If there is no higher law beyond man, then man is his own god . . . when you choose your authority, you choose your god, and when you look for your law, there is your god."[16]

America must choose her god. Either it will be the courts with their arbitrary laws based on the pressures of the moment or it will be the Supreme Lawgiver before and to whom we must all give account. Only He is qualified to unite law and morality and thereby enable us to judge the conflicting whims of human courts.

A god we must have. Which one shall we choose?

16. R. J. Rushdoony, *Law and Liberty* (Fairfax, Va.: Thoburn, 1971), p. 33.

5

THE MYTH THAT MORALITY CANNOT BE LEGISLATED

Secular humanists would like us to believe that they are broad-minded, pluralistic, and neutral in moral matters. They are opposed to censorship, sectarianism, and intolerance. The news media has done a successful job of getting the American people to believe that it is the so-called right-wing religious fanatics who are seeking to "impose their morality on society." According to the October 8, 1984 issue of *Time* magazine, 77 percent of the American people believe that it is all right for religious leaders to speak out on social issues, but 72 percent believe that religious groups should not try to impose their teachings on others through the political process. Clearly, the media has been successful in making us appear guilty of legislating morality and in implying that the secularists do not.

But all laws are an imposition of someone's morality. That is why the statement "You cannot legislate morality," as it stands, is absurd. Obviously we cannot legislate what a person thinks, but all actions *in principle* are capable of being curbed by law. To be fair, we must acknowledge that those who use this slogan often mean that the law cannot interfere with one's private morality. But we do have laws regarding compulsory education, restrictions on the sale of drugs, laws against cruelty to animals, and laws against incest.

Are secularists more tolerant than Christians? Both have a desire to see their form of morality accepted by the public at large. And presently in America, the secularists are using the state to impose their morality on society as a whole. When humanism is weak it cries out for tolerance and freedom, when it becomes strong it turns into totalitarianism. In 1934 Christopher Dawson predicted, "The great danger that we have to meet is not the danger of violent persecution but rather that of the crushing out of religion from modern life by the sheer weight of state-inspired public opinion and by the mass organization of society on a purely secular basis."[1]

Secularism will use every means at its disposal to crush opposition to its ideology. And as Harvey Cox saw so well, it is most deceptive when it pretends to be neutral. "Secularism, on the other hand, is the name (of) an ideology, a new closed-world view which functions very much like a new religion . . . it must be especially checked where it pretends not to be a world view but nonetheless seeks to impose its ideology through the organs of the state."[2]

How is secular humanism imposing its morality on others? It does so through the media, the schools, and the courts.

1. Quoted in William Bentley Ball, "Religious Liberty in 1984: Perils and Promises," *Christian Legal Society Quarterly* 5, no. 1 (1984):4.
2. Harvey Cox, *The Secular City* (London: SCM, 1965), p. 21.

THE MEDIA

Jesus Christ taught that neutrality was impossible. He explained, "He who is not with Me is against Me; and he who does not gather with Me scatters" (Matthew 12:30). Christians have never claimed to be neutral, but often the secularists lay claim to such a distinction. But of course moral neutrality is a myth.

According to a 1982 survey of 240 journalists and broadcasters at the most influential media outlets, 54 percent placed themselves to the left of the political center, compared to only 19 percent who chose the right side of the spectrum. According to Robert Lichter and Stanley Rothman, 56 percent of those interviewed agreed that American economic exploitation has contributed to Third-World poverty. By a 3 to 1 ratio they believe that Third-World nations would be better off without the assistance they have received from the West. More telling is the fact that 90 percent agree that a woman has a right to decide for herself to have an abortion.[3]

In a word, the media is biased, often interested in shaping attitudes as well as reporting the news. Many of those with influential media positions wish to get their liberal agenda across to the nation.

And how is this accomplished? First of all, through benign neglect of the Christian position on social issues. There is a clear intention to keep Christian thinking out of the mainstream of political life. Just try getting them to publish a story that does not agree with the humanists' viewpoint.

A few examples: In May of 1982 Jane Fonda's exercise book was number one on the *New York Times'*

---

3. Franky Schaeffer, *A Time for Anger* (Westchester, Ill.: Crossway, 1982), p. 27.

best seller list. Yet that month Fonda's book sold only half as many copies as Francis Schaeffer's *Christian Manifesto*, which was not even listed. Papers such as the *New York Times* will not list books of a Christian view point regardless of how many are sold. They use the smoke screen that religious books are in a special class and hence do not deserve a review. But if a cookbook sold an overwhelming number of copies it would be reviewed even though it is a specialty item. Only religious bigotry of a most unsophisticated kind can account for the censorship exercised by such newspapers.[4]

Most American newspapers carry stories on divorce, child molesting, and bad marriages. Because one half of all divorces are caused by adultery, and in keeping with the statistics that those who are sexually faithful in their marriages live more happily, one would think newspapers could carry occasional articles on the benefits of marital fidelity. But such articles are rejected out of hand and labeled "puritanical" or "narrow-minded." In other words, one must often assume the propriety of immorality before he can write an article for a magazine or newspaper. Whether the topic is sex, abortion, or homosexuality, the Christian viewpoint is so often screened out by the media. As Franky Schaeffer has written, "They want us to feel guilty and somewhat inferior, as if our views are biased and bigoted, while their views—the views of the secular, humanistic elite—are somehow more enlightened."[5]

Second, when the media cannot neglect the Christian viewpoint, it often uses loaded terminology to put

4. Cal Thomas, *Book Burning* (Westchester, Ill.: Crossway, 1983), p. 105. Thomas explodes the myth that Christians are censors, and shows how secularists seek to muzzle all those who do not agree with their viewpoint.
5. Franky Schaeffer, "The Myth of Neutrality," *Moody Monthly,* November 1980, p. 20.

such a viewpoint in the worst possible light. It refers to "right-wing fundamentalism" or "puritanism." Other adjectives might be "sectarianism" or "mindless orthodoxy." All such terms convey to the reader the notion that Christians are uneducated religious bigots who are not worth listening to. Just recently there was a program on television that likened the Moral Majority to Nazism with its brainwashing techniques. It showed a picture of a bonfire with books being burned, implying that this is what all Christians would like to do. However, as Cal Thomas has shown clearly in his book entitled *Book Burning,* the label "bookburners" applies more directly to the secular humanist than it does to the Moral Majority or other Christian groups.

When Francis Schaeffer's film *Whatever Happened to the Human Race?* was shown on a television station in Washington, proabortionists exerted all the influence they could to prevent it from being aired. The pluralism and openmindedness that they verbally espoused was not practiced. After the film was shown, the *Washington Post* ran an article entitled "No Matter How Moving, Show Still Propaganda." Thus what the media did was to ridicule the program with loaded terminology.[6]

The words of Cal Thomas deserve careful reading:

> The modern censors first manipulate and redefine language in a way that makes any challenge to their rule-setting appear intolerant and narrow minded. Whatever they say, no matter how one-dimensional, no matter how blasphemous or scatalogical, must be treated with profound reverence. But God help anyone who utters the mildest protest or suggests that an alternative view should also be presented. Should such a person transgress and trespass on the holy ground of the mass media and academia, the full weight of their

6. Schaeffer, *A Time for Anger,* p. 30.

elitist condemnation will come crashing down around them like multi-targeted warheads. He or she will be dubbed (choose one or more, please) a censorer, a bigot, an Ayatollah, a fundamentalist, an underminer of the first amendment, a religious fanatic, a puritan, an ignoramous, or a bookburner.[7]

One editor admitted that the only religious news story the press likes to do is a scandal. All other religious viewpoints are smothered by the censors who are insistent that only one point of view be presented.

THE SCHOOLS

Years ago in America academic freedom meant that different viewpoints could be presented in the classroom. Pluralism, the belief that there could be more than one position on an issue, was championed. But today the first amendment, which guarantees freedom of expression, has been taken away from our teachers and they are forced to parrot one viewpoint only, that of secular humanism.

Despite all the evidence that contradicts evolution, it *must* be taught in the schools. The existence of God or of the human soul cannot be presented as a possible explanation for the existence of the universe and mankind. All education must be based on atheism, materialism, and relativism. This is really no different from Communist countries where the views of the state must be taught and all other viewpoints suppressed.

To see how censorship works in our schools, let's contrast the way the press handled Mel and Norma Gabler versus other textbook reviewers. The Texas State Board of Education allows the public to review books before selection, and because Texas is a huge

7. Thomas, pp. 15-16.

client, publishers compete for business. The Gablers
have been reading books for more than twenty years,
and they submit comments regarding textbooks under consideration. According to their testimony, the
schools have gradually censored "practically all
books which uphold, promote, or teach the basic values upon which our nation was founded."

All around the country the Gablers have been criticized in the newspapers. They have been called
"censors," "God-appointed watch dogs," and so on.
Yet virtually every social group has submitted similar
critiques of the textbooks in Texas. Even the National
Organization for the Reform of Marijuana Laws sub-
mits reviews. Feminists campaign in full force trying to
promote books that espouse their liberal causes.

Why are the Gablers branded as censors but the
other groups are not?

According to an article in *Redbook* magazine,
Vicky Worsham, the divorced mother of two girls
aged 13 and 10, was eager to impress upon her own
daughters that they must take responsibility for themselves. She and as many feminists as she could muster
appeared in Austin before the textbook committee to
testify against the acquiring of books she thought dis-
criminated or gave an unrealistic view of women. In
the past, she was the head of the National Organization for Women's educational task force in Texas.[8]

Can you imagine an article in a newspaper that
would call her a censor? Of course not. She would be
considered pluralistic and open minded. Yet she and
her friends are doing exactly what the Gablers have
done. Both are exercising their legitimate privileges
in the democratic process. But one is called names by
the press and the other is not.

In some school districts the textbooks are censored

8. Ibid., pp. 94-95.

carefully to make sure they contain no teaching about God. Because of the novel understanding of church and state, it is believed that nothing can be taught that is religious. If that isn't censorship, what is it?

When sex education is taught in a "how-to approach" it is called "value clarification." Or the course is considered to be "value free." This is presented as pluralism, the academic freedom that is so highly cherished. But if a course were taught that stressed sex within marriage alone, it would be branded as puritanical, one-dimensional, narrow-minded, and out of step with the times. In other words, immorality is always broad mindedness; sexual fidelity is closed mindedness. Permissivists bristle when the other side wants equal time. Only when a course is slanted toward the humanistic agenda is it considered a valid approach to pluralism.

When a book entitled *How to Have Sex with Children* was confiscated by the police in Chicago, several demonstrators marched with pickets protesting the violation of the first amendment. In other words, they believed pornographers should have unlimited privileges in publishing whatever they please. And yet, it is not legal to have a period for prayer, or to teach creationism in our schools. When the humanists speak of open mindedness they mean only that they allow some variation within their own viewpoint. As columnist George Will put it so ably, "And it is, by now, a scandal beyond irony that thanks to the energetic litigation of 'civil liberties' fanatics, pornographers enjoy expansive first amendment protection while first graders in a nativity play are said to violate first amendment values."[9]

In recent decades the church in America has been

9. George Will, *Washington Post,* 23 December 1979, p. E-7.

tolerant of differing views, allowing both options to be presented to the American public. But the humanists do not express the same tolerance they expect from us. While speaking about pluralism they fanatically censor all religious influence and insist that their view alone is worthy of a hearing. Their bigotry rivals that of the most rabid religious zealot.

Dr. Pierce of Harvard University, when addressing 2,000 teachers in Denver said:

> Every child in America who enters school at the age of five is mentally ill, because he comes to school with allegiance toward our elected officials, toward our founding fathers, toward our institutions, toward the preservation of this form of government . . . patriotism, nationalism, sovereignity . . . all of that proves that children are sick, because the truly well individual is one who has rejected all of those things and is what I would call the true international child of the future.[10]

In some schools students are asked to write suicide notes and even samples are presented to stimulate them to complete the assignment. At other times students are asked to respond to intimate questions about sexuality such as, "How often do you think that a teen should have sex?" or "What form of sexual activity do you enjoy the most?" Here again the real agenda is to strip the child of all moral or spiritual values and to encourage immorality as normal behavior. In one classroom the teacher began by asking, "How many of you children hate your parents?" Only three hands were raised. But after her effective presentation she asked the same question, and this time all but three hands were raised. One is reminded of George Orwell's *1984* where he says that the family

10. Quoted in William M. Bowen, *Globalism: America's Demise* (Lafayette, La.: Huntington House, 1984), pp. 19-20.

need not be actually abolished, but the children are systematically turned against their parents and taught to spy on them and report their deviation. The family had become in effect the extension of the "thought police." Farfetched as it may sound, it seems to be happening in some of our schools.

To quote Christopher Dawson once more:

> The new state will be universal and omni-competent. It will mold and guide the life of its citizens from the cradle to the grave. It will not tolerate any interference with its educational functions by any sectarian organization, even though the latter is based on religious convictions. And this is the more serious, since the introduction of psychology into education has made the schoolmaster a spiritual guide as well as a trainer of the mind. In fact it seems as though the school of the future must increasingly usurp the functions that the church exercised in the past, and that the teaching profession will take the place of the clergy as the spiritual power of the future.[11]

THE LAW

The secular state always pushes its values on society through the courts. Law is a social phenomenon that holds society together. Laws should strike a balance between the general welfare of the state and the freedom of the individual. For example, whereas there should be laws that allow parents to teach their children, there should also be laws against child abuse. To maintain such a balance between freedom and form is a difficult task. The question of how far the state has the right to encroach on the lives of its citizens is not always easily answered.

What is clear, however, is that no law is "neutral."

---

11. Quoted in Ball, *Christian Legal Society Quarterly,* pp. 4-5.

Every law imposes some form of morality on society. Thus abortionists impose their morality on the unborn; homosexuals want to have their views taught to all children in the public school classrooms, and atheists want religious influence excluded from public life. All of this is being done by passing laws that would limit freedom of religion, freedom of speech, and in the case of abortion, freedom for the unborn to live.

It is simply not true to say that the religious right wants to impose its values on society but the secular humanist does not. The courts are forcing their secular values on society whether the public likes it or not.

In an article in *Newsweek*, September 21, 1981, Jerry Falwell spoke specifically to the question of whether or not morality can be legislated. His statement quoted here should be carefully read:

> Let's remember that all law is the imposition of someone's morality to the exclusion of someone else's morality. We have laws against murder, rape, incest, cannibalism and stealing. No doubt there are murderers, rapists, practitioners of incest, cannibals and thieves who are upset that their "rights" have been denied. But in order to provide for the common defense and promote the general welfare, it was deemed necessary to pass such laws.[12]

Neutrality is a myth. Politicians, in an attempt to remain "neutral," tell us they are personally opposed to abortion but would never dream of imposing their values on society. A question to ask them is, Why are you personally against abortion? Is it perhaps because abortion is the taking of an innocent human life? If so, how does this sound? "I personally would never gas a Jew, but I have no right to impose my moral judgment on the Nazis. I don't think that the

12. Jerry Falwell, "My Turn," *Newsweek*, 21 September 1981.

courts have the right to reach into someone's private gas chamber and legislate morality."

Christ was right when He taught that it is not possible to serve two masters; either we gather with Him or we scatter. Jesus said that a kingdom divided against itself would not be able to stand. In the conflict, one must choose sides. Neutrality is not possible.

The question is not whether public policy will be influenced by religion in America, the real question is, What religion? Whose morality will be legislated?

At this point the evangelical Christian has been more honest than the humanist. *We do not claim to be neutral.* We stand against abortion, radical feminism, and gay rights. We are opposed to censorship in the schools, and are in favor of free speech and pluralism. We confess we are either helping to reverse the dangerous trends in society or we are contributing to them by our negligence. To claim neutrality is to give ground to the enemy.

The ancient Greeks had a race in which a man would put one of his feet on one horse and the other foot on a second horse and then try to ride the horses while he was standing up. It worked quite well until the horses separated, and then the rider had a decision to make.

Whether you have signed up or not, we are in a battle that is being fought around us. The question is not Should something be done? but rather *What* should be done? Our attention will be given to these questions in the final chapters of this book.

6

THE MYTH THAT
THE ROLES OF MEN
AND WOMEN ARE
INTERCHANGEABLE

The proposed Equal Rights Amendment (ERA) to the United States Constitution died in 1982. But the concept of equality for men and women is still very much alive in the minds of millions of Americans. The amendment reads simply, "Equality of life under the law shall not be denied or abridged by the United States or by any state on account of sex."

What could possibly be wrong with this statement? Isn't it time we abolished discrimination? Aren't women entitled to equal rights? Don't they deserve equal pay for equal work?

On the surface it seems that every Christian should be in favor of the ERA. If we take seriously the biblical teaching that women are created in the image of God they certainly are entitled to equal rights.

Reading a book such as *Radical Feminism* helps us better understand the legitimate concerns that women have. They have been used by men; they have been treated as inferior; they have been exploited by pornography and the selfishness of males. To read feminist literature is to sense the anger and frustration that many women face. Some think the ERA would put an end to such abuses.

Yet behind this proposed constitutional amendment lies a deception. If ERA had been ratified it would likely have brought about a sweeping restructuring of society. There is reason to believe that it represents one of the most devastating attacks on the family and morality in general. It is not too much to say that this amendment would likely destroy America as we know it.

The media has carefully diverted attention from the real goals of the radical feminists who back this proposal now that it has been resubmitted to Congress. Repeatedly we have heard that the amendment simply means women would have equal pay for equal work. But as a result of the Equal Employment Opportunity Act of 1972, women already are guaranteed equal pay for equal work. The ERA would make no contribution to rectify such injustices. When Phyllis Schlafly debated a leading congressional proponent of ERA, former Congresswoman Martha Griffiths, Schlafly made the point that the ERA will do absolutely nothing for women in the area of employment. Griffiths replied, "I never claimed it would." Thus at least some ERA supporters acknowledged that they are striving for different goals.

What is wrong with ERA? The problem lies with the definition of the word *equality.* The feminists interpret it to mean that women would have equality so far as their roles are concerned—that is, the place of women in society would be interchangeable with that of men. Whatever men do, women would be able to do. *All gender-based roles would be abolished.* Toward this end, the media, greatly influenced by the avant-garde mood of the feminists, is attempting to dismantle the traditional concept of what a woman should do and who she should be. Gone are the days when femininity and motherhood were looked upon with respect.

A listener to Dr. James Dobson's radio program "Focus on the Family" wrote saying that she had discovered thousands of books had been taken from her public library. Investigation showed that these books were the ones based on the traditional roles of father and mother—father the breadwinner with mother staying at home to rear the children. Now the shelves were stocked with books that portrayed the contemporary woman who pursues her career outside the home. The children are at a day-care center and the father is equally involved in their upbringing. The woman portrayed in that manner is in every respect equal to a man.

The radical feminists have clearly defined goals they wish to achieve. In the process they believe they must smash the traditional understanding of marriage, children, and religion so that equality can be brought about. The woman's role is being redefined.

And what does *equality* mean to the feminists? Here are several goals they would like to achieve.

GOALS OF FEMINISTS

TO DESTROY THE BONDAGE OF MARRIAGE

The feminists believe that marriage represents a hierarchy—the woman is in submission to the man, who is the head of the home. Since marriage reinforces the male and female roles, such servitude must be destroyed. As Bonnie Kreps put it, "We must fight the corrupt notion we now call 'love' which is based on control of another rather than on love for the

growth of another; we must fight the institutionaliza-
tion of the oppression of women—especially the institution of marriage."[1]

A group called The Feminists drew up a declaration that was ratified on August 8, 1969. One of the
rules was that no more than ⅓ of the membership
could be either legally married or living with a man.
Why? Three reasons were given: (1) marriage is in-
herently inequitable whether formal or informal,
(2) marriage formalizes the persecution of women,
and (3) the document declares, "We consider the rejection of this institution both in theory and in practice
a primary mark of the radical feminist."[2]

What has happened to love? Traditionally society
believed that a man and woman could love each
other and seek one another's highest good. But in a
chapter entitled "The Feminists: A Political Organization to Annihilate Sex Roles" the author says, "We must
destroy love (an institution by definition), which is
generally recognized as approval and acceptance.
Love promotes vulnerability, dependence, possessive-
ness, susceptibility to pain and prevents the full development of woman's human potential by directing all
her energies outward in the interest of others."[3]

But doesn't a woman have sexual needs that can be
best met by a man? Some feminists insist that women
should find their sexual fulfillment in masturbation,
thus becoming totally independent. Others teach that
lesbianism is the logical life-style to adopt because a
relationship with other women would eliminate the
need to be submissive to men. Ti-Grace Atkinson is

1. Bonnie Kreps, "Radical Feminism I," in Anne Koedt, Ellen Levine, and
   Anita Rapone, eds., *Radical Feminism* (New York: Quadrangle, 1973),
   p. 239.
2. "The Feminists: A Political Organization to Annihilate Sex Roles," in
   Radical Feminism, p. 374.
3. Ibid., p. 375.

quoted as saying, "Feminism is the theory; lesbianism is the practice."[4]

Clearly the feminists believe that the end of the institution of marriage is a necessary condition for the liberation of women. They affirm that women should be encouraged to leave their husbands and not to live individually with men. Shiela Cronan speaks for many when she writes, "Since marriage constitutes slavery for women, it is clear that the Women's Movement must concentrate on attacking this institution. Freedom for women cannot be won without the abolition of marriage."[5]

Later in this chapter we will briefly outline a biblical response to the proposals of the radical feminists. For now it is enough to realize that the destruction of marriage is hardly the answer for the legitimate grievances many women have. The proposed cure is worse than the disease. Yet despite the implications for society, to destroy marriage is "a primary mark of the radical feminist."

FREEDOM FROM THE BURDEN OF CHILDREN

The feminists believe that there can be no equality as long as the woman is a homemaker. In the *Communist Manifesto* Karl Marx stressed that the family system is the result of capitalism, which divides society into classes. Hence the Communist Party in 1919 vowed to win equality for women. Lenin's stated goal was that there should be no distinction between men and women as far as their rights and duties were concerned. As women become involved in the means of production the children are reared by the state.

4. Anne Koedt, "Lesbianism and Feminism," in *Radical Feminism*, p. 246.
5. Sheila Cronan, "Marriage," in *Radical Feminism*, p. 219.

Consistent with this view of equality the radical feminists write, "Childrearing to the extent to which it is necessary is the responsibility of all. Children are part of society but they should not be possessed by anyone . . . marriage and the family must be eliminated."[6]

A survey of feminist literature shows the close connection between liberation and socialism. For example, Linda Jenness in her book *Socialism and the Fight for Women's Rights* argues that historically socialism and feminism were synonymous, and she quotes Marx, Engels, and Lenin to prove her point. She also explains how the socialist-feminists change society by concentrating on equal pay, child care, education, and sexual freedom. The strategy is to exploit legitimate grievances and then offer a Marxist solution.

At a women's conference sponsored by the National Organization for Women in Normal, Illinois, China was extolled as an example of a country where women had achieved equality. In that country the state rears the children, the women work. The women of Cuba are also used as examples of liberation. There is an unbreakable bond between feminism and socialistic Marxism.

Friedrich Engels, who along with Marx wrote the *Communist Manifesto,* said, "The care and education of children becomes a public affair; society looks after all children alike, whether they are legitimate or not."[7] He goes on to say that only then will a girl not have to fear the consequences of giving herself to a man she loves; hence sexual liberation will be achieved. Not surprisingly, at the Houston Conference for Women sponsored by NOW there was a call for

6. *Radical Feminism*, pp. 375-76.
7. Friedrich Engels, "The Origin of the Family," in Alice S. Rossi, ed., *The Feminist Papers* (New York: Columbia U., 1973), p. 488.

federally funded day-care centers that would operate twenty-four hours a day, seven days a week. Only
by putting the responsibility of children on society as
a whole, it was argued, could women be free. Thus
the state was asked to take the responsibility for the
rearing of children. Marxists would add that the state
should have this responsibility so that the proper indoctrination of children would be assured.

Sometimes Christian women have been heard to
say, "I'm opposed to abortion, but I am for the ERA."
This is contradictory. Betty Friedan argues the point
clearly: Although conception requires both male and
female, only the female has the responsibility of car-
rying the child to term; therefore it is discrimination to
force her to have responsibility for the unborn child. If
the roles of men and women are equal, the woman
must have the right to kill her unborn baby.

Understandably, nothing positive is written about
children in feminist literature. At best, mothers are
taught how they can teach their daughters to live
independently of men. Children are almost always
considered to be an obstacle to a woman's right to
become a part of the work force outside the home. As
James Dobson has observed, "Kids have been per-
ceived as an imposition, a nuisance, and a drain on
the world's natural resources."

Who would have believed that the time would
come when mothers who stayed home would be ridiculed and treated with disrespect? There was a time
when rearing children was an honorable profession
that could be done without apology. But today those
who do so are stigmatized as old-fashioned or out of
step with the times. For fear of being considered out of
step with society, young pregnant women are afraid
to tell their friends that they plan to quit work when
the baby comes.

THE SUPRESSION OF RELIGION

Because the Judeo-Christian ethic cherishes the family, religion is seen as another force that must be destroyed if the family is to be properly dismantled. Consistent with Marxism the feminists write, "Political institutions such as religion, because they are based on philosophies of hierarchical orders and reinforce male oppression of females must be destroyed."[8]

Equality has far-reaching implications for our churches. As indicated in a previous chapter, in 1983 Bob Jones University lost its tax-exempt status. The university admits blacks, but it does not admit students of mixed marriages or permit interracial dating. This teaching, the school maintains, is not based on racial discrimination but on religious grounds. The administration believes the races are to be kept separate.

Although many of us strongly oppose the position of Bob Jones University, the Internal Revenue Service had no right to withhold tax exemption from the school. The Supreme Court did not question the sincerity of the religious convictons of the university, but based its decision on the grounds that to receive tax exemption an organization must (1) serve a public purpose and (2) not act contrary to public policy. As Kenneth S. Kantzer said, "This ruling will be used to force all religious, charitable, and private educational organizations to confine their activity to positions approved by the general populace on pain of losing their tax exemption."[9]

NOW opposes the right of churches to make any differentiation between men and women. It advocates sexual equality in seminary and already is fighting to deny tax exemption to churches that dis-

8. *Radical Feminism*, p. 377.
9. Kenneth S. Kantzer, "The Bob Jones Decision: A Dangerous Precedent," *Christianity Today*, 2 September 1983, p. 14.

criminate between men and women on religious grounds. It is not difficult to see how the refusal to ordain women and homosexuals could soon be interpreted as "contrary to public policy."

Feminism, then, is based on a socialistic view of equality that is incompatible with religious freedom. By denying the existence of gender-based roles, it tramples on important distinctions inherent in Christian values in the home and in the church.

OFFICIAL RECOGNITION OF HOMOSEXUALITY

Some of the strongest support for the "push for equality" comes from the homosexual community. The argument is that a law that permits a man to marry a woman, but denies him the right to marry another man, is discriminatory. Thus lesbian and homosexual marriages could be legalized if ERA were ratified.

Jean O'Leary, head of the Gay Task Force, has written a paper calling for the incorporation of homosexuality into every subject taught at school. She wants children to grow up believing that homosexuality is an alternate "sexual preference," and morally is no different from heterosexuality.

Homosexuals are also fighting to gain special status as a minority group. They are anxious to create a favored class of people who would gain an unfair position in the job market. An employer would have to hire a homosexual even if he passed over more qualified candidates, lest he be taken to court in a discrimination suit.

No one doubts that homosexuals deserve the protection of the law, but do they have the right to impose their life-style on society under the guise of "equality?" To insist that homosexuality must be taught in the schools as "an alternate sexual preference," and to accuse church leaders of discrimination when they refuse to ordain homosexuals, is to violate the moral convictions of millions of Americans. The next step would be to say that Christians cannot denounce homosexuality as sin, since such distinctions would be discrimination.

Equality sounds like a worthy concept, but all too often it entails the obliteration of legitimate moral distinctions. Homosexuality is not only contrary to the Bible, but violates natural law as well. To take what is unnatural and try to have society accept it as natural is to infringe on the moral sensibilities of the general populace.

On March 26, 1985, the Supreme Court affirmed an appellate court ruling that struck down an Oklahoma law permitting public school districts to fire teachers who openly advocated homosexuality. What this means in practical terms is that homosexual teachers can flaunt their life-style in the classroom without any protest from parents or teachers.

Just think of the implications if all gender-based roles were interchangeable. The ERA, if it were ever ratified, could require no segregation of the sexes in prisons, reform schools, public schools, college dormitories, hospital rooms, and other public facilities. Though ERA supporters have sometimes scoffed at such implications, in 1972 the late Senator Sam Ervin suggested that the ERA have some changes in wording. Among those suggested were that the amendment not be interpreted to mean separate public facilities would be abolished, or that women would be drafted into the military for exactly the same combat duties as men. But those proposals were rejected.

Because there could be no law that pertains to women but not to men, prostitution could immediately be legalized. In a western state that adopted a basic ERA position in its state laws, women who were swimming topless at the beach could not be arrested for indecent exposure. After all, you cannot invoke a law that pertains to them unless it applies to men too.

When faced with these difficulties, ERA supporters repeatedly tell us that no one can predict how this amendment would be applied by the courts. But in saying that it would be up to the courts to make such crucial decisions, the ERA supporters are perfectly content to turn these sensitive moral issues over to what one critic has called "the least democratic institution of our republic." Though we cannot predict accurately how the amendment might be interpreted, we do know that it would be unconstitutional to pass any law that differentiates between men and women.

THE BIBLE AND EQUALITY

One of the most positive results of the feminist movement is that the Christian community has had to reevaluate what the Bible has to say about the roles of men and women. It is easy enough to condemn the extreme views of the radical feminists, but we must ask ourselves what solution we have to offer for the injustices women often experience. Let's not turn a deaf ear to the hurts that underlie the shrill voices of reform.

To begin, let us confess with shame that men have often unfairly dominated women in the name of Christianity. Because the Bible teaches that man is the head of the home, and that the wife should be in subjection to his authority, men (yes, even Christian men) have often taken unfair advantage of a woman's creativity and freedom.

The diagnosis made by the feminists may be quite correct, but the cure is disastrous. To insist that marriage, the family, and love be destroyed to achieve radical freedom would only increase the alienation between men and women and cause even greater emotional trauma in the lives of children. Recent studies indicate that the level of emotional damage done to children as a result of their parents' divorce has often been underestimated. By smashing marriage, the foundation of society would be dismantled.

Furthermore, the ERA would not rectify the injustices done against women but perhaps even increase them. It is reasonable to assume that a husband would no longer be required to support his family because women would have equal financial responsibility for themselves and their children. If a divorce occurred she would be forced out of her home because child support would be shared.

So what should our response as Christians be? First, we must emphasize the total biblical teaching regarding husband-wife relationships. True, the wife is to be submissive to her husband, but the husband in turn is to love his wife as Christ loved the church. He is responsible for putting her needs above his own. In practical terms this means that if there is enough money for only one suit of clothes, his wife should be preferred; if his job requires that he be separated from his family more often than his wife can tolerate, he should trust God for a different vocation. His goal should not be to make himself successful but rather to make his wife satisfied.

The husband is responsible to provide for his family financially and if he does not he has denied the faith and is worse than an unbeliever (1 Timothy 5:8). God holds him accountable for how he provides for his wife and family.

As the head of the home, the father has ultimate responsibility for his wife and family. However that certainly does not mean he makes all the decisions. There should be shared responsibility within the confines of the various roles. To be a male chauvinist is to accept a distortion of the biblical teaching.

Second, we must realize that the Bible allows for the mother to pursue a career, at least as long as she operates from home base like the mother in Proverbs

31. She is commended for her creativity and resourcefulness. And certainly a married woman who either has no children or whose children have grown, can be free to pursue a career if she and her husband agree on the matter.

We must educate mothers so that they understand that God has given them the most important task in the world. No success in business will ever make up for the failure to rear children for the glory of God; success in the home will always compensate for the lack of opportunities in the business world. After all, our most important resource is our children—they are the only commodity God has given us that we can take with us to heaven.

Our influence must be felt wherever there are legitimate injustices, either inside the home, the church, or society. If a woman is underpaid simply because of her gender, let us be the first to cry "foul." And if tax laws favor men and penalize women, let's use all of our resources to get the laws changed.

The point is that we must understand how sin has affected the relationship between men and women. Sin causes a husband to treat his wife unfairly, under the guise of her need to "submit." Sin causes women to crave total freedom from any kind of marriage restraints. Sin causes one marriage partner to betray another, either through extramarital sexual relationships, verbal abuse, or insensitivity to the partner's needs. Only the humble recognition of personal sin, with a turning to Christ for forgiveness, can begin to alleviate the selfishness and guilt that so often ruptures marriage relationships.

Sin always builds barriers between husbands and wives, parents and children. Rather than strengthening these walls, we must seek to demolish them. Forgiveness, love, and sensitivity are the places to start.

The Bible teaches that men and women are different without being fundamentally unequal. Each has rather well-defined roles that are necessary for the orderly function of society and for the training of children. Women are equal in several ways: First, they are equal in *creation.* Even though Eve was created for Adam she was an equal partner, made in the image of God. From the standpoint of her intelligence and importance as an individual there is no distinction.

Women are also equal in *salvation.* Paul wrote "There is neither Jew nor Greek, there is neither slave nor free man, there is neither male nor female; for you are all one in Christ Jesus" (Galatians 3:28). Clearly women have the same opportunities as men in their relationship with God. They have often benefited more from spiritual opportunities than men. Just look at any prayer meeting, Bible class, or volunteer project in the church and you will see that women are usually more committed than men. They often take spiritual leadership by default because men are too proud to seek a vital relationship with God.

Finally, women are equal in *accountability.* Both Adam and Eve were judged because of their sin. Even though Adam was to protect his wife from evil influence, he did not do so. Both he and his wife were held accountable.

The biblical understanding is "equal but different." It's not an equality that would substitute one role for another, but an equality as persons before God with different functions in the home and in society.

Some time ago the World Council of Churches released a Biblical Lectionary that omitted all gender-based terms. God is no longer referred to as *He.* This pronoun has been taken out of the text and a noun substituted. "For God so loved the world that God gave God's only child . . ." Such rebellion against the male/female distinction in Scripture is, at root, anger against God. It is He that has made us male and fe-male and has established the boundaries wherein we should serve and work. To disregard these differences is to invite the disintegration of society. Our children will be raised by the state, and the values of marital fidelity and love will be laid to rest. In place of these values will be self-serving individualism, bitterness, and despair.

7

THE MYTH THAT
A FETUS IS NOT A BABY

Some time ago, a father threw his newborn son against the floor of the delivery room, killing the infant. In what has to be one of the greatest moral contradictions of all time, this man was charged with murder, even though the baby could have been put to death legally the day before.

Any morally sensitive person must ask Why? Why is a man charged with murder for an act that could have been done the previous day without penalty? Admittedly, throwing a baby against a floor is barbaric, but is it *in principle* any different from killing an infant with the abortionist's saline injection, which burns the infant's skin while it struggles for life? Even more gruesome is the spectacle of using a suction device that tears the body of the developing baby apart, sucking the "product of conception" into a jar. Such abortions are performed on preborn infants that are viable (they can exist outside of the womb on their own) to ensure that they will not be born alive.

Even proabortionists see the logic: If a mother may

legally choose to destroy her child within the womb,
obviously she can destroy it outside the womb. Since
biologically there is no distinction between a fetus
and a baby, abortion inevitably leads to infanticide.
Metaphysically the two acts are indistinguishable.
Proabortionist Peter Singer of Monash University in
Australia wrote in the journal *Pediatrics* that those
who believe in the sanctity of human life argue very
plausibly "that the location of the fetus/infant—inside
or outside the womb—cannot make a crucial difference to its moral status."[1]

Today 4,300 preborn babies will be legally put to
death under the protection of the Supreme Court's
1973 decision in *Roe* v. *Wade*. Back in those days
abortion was presented as the last act of a desperate
woman. But today 97 percent of all abortions take
place simply for convenience. Abortion has become
the nation's means of birth control.

The hidden assumption in the *Roe* v. *Wade* decision
is that man is essentially an animal who has come up
through the evolutionary continuum. Peter Singer,
who is quoted above, wrote, "We can no longer base
our ethics on the idea that human beings are a special form of creation made in the image of God and
singled out from all other animals."[2] In other words,
man is not only an animal, but he is not even special
among animals.

To starve a baby because he is either unwanted or
handicapped is just as reasonable in an atheistic
world as is killing a deformed pig. After all, we are
but animals, a bundle of cells, a collection of molecules that has no special significance. A recent report
indicated that babies' bodies are sold by the bag.

1. Peter Singer, *Pediatrics* 72, no. 1 (July 1983):129.
2. Ibid.

They are used in some cosmetics and for experimentation. In one general hospital the sale of preborn babies brought in $68,000 in a ten-year period.[3]

The high Court justified its abortion ruling by appealing to paganism. Justice Harry Blackmun, author of the 64-page document, stated that objection to abortion comes mainly from two sources, the oath of Hippocrates and Christianity. Because the oath specifically forbids abortion, the Court did wrestle with its influence, but concluded that the oath did not correspond to the general opinion of the ancient world. Blackmun wrote, "Ancient religions did not bar abortion." As for Christianity's influence, it was apparently dismissed by the Court because of the separation of church and state. In effect, the Court omitted two thousand years of the Judeo-Christian influence and reached back into paganism to find a basis for its moral judgment.

The Court made its decision with the understanding that laws could be made independently of the Constitution, based on the necessities of the moment. Though the Court justified its decision on grounds of the "right to privacy," this was nothing more than a facade in making up a woman's right to have an abortion. Justice Byron White, who dissented on the vote said, "I find nothing in the language or history of the constitution to support the Court's judgment. The Court simply fashions and announces a new constitutional right. As an exercise of raw judicial power, the Court perhaps had authority to do what it does today, but in my view its judgment is an improvident and extravagant exercise of the power of judicial review."

In its decision the Court said that a woman could even have an abortion during the third trimester of

3. *The Christian Activist* 1, no. 2 (Summer 1984):11.

pregnancy to preserve her life or health. In a decision made the same day, *Doe* v. *Bolton*, the Court defined *health* in the broadest medical context, such as psychological, emotional, and family considerations. This gave women the right to have an abortion up to the point of birth as long as the woman needs it for her "emotional well-being." As Justice White put it, today abortion is legal in America "for any reason or for no reason."

Thus the Court exercised its raw power and passed a law that was neither voted on by the people of the United States nor enacted by our legislatures. As a result of its arrogant disregard for moral values, the Court invalidated all abortion laws in fifty states and made its will supreme. As a result, more than 18 million unborn children have had their lives snuffed out—ten times the total number of Americans lost in all of our nation's wars.

In a subsequent decision, *Planned Parenthood* v. *Danforth* (1976), the Court ruled that the consent of the father of the unborn child or that of the grandparents was not necessary for a girl to have an abortion. Then in June of 1983, the Court struck down informed consent laws that required that a woman be fully assessed of the specifics of her abortion surgery (including risks, alternatives, and the state of her child's development). These rulings established abortion as a fundamental and absolute right.

Today abortion is big business. With 1.5 million abortions each year, costing an average of $350 each, abortion clinics make tens of thousands of dollars daily. When business is slack, those who admit pregnant women do all they can to encourage an abortion regardless of the medical or emotional consequences.

What does the Bible say? Here are three biblical

propositions that will guide us in understanding the status of the fetus.

(1) *All persons are special creations.*

Genesis 1:26 reads, "Then God said, 'Let Us make man in Our image, according to Our likeness.' " Verse 27 continues, "And God created man in His own image, in the image of God He created him; male and female He created them." What does it mean to be created in God's image? Although we share the world with animals, the human race has uniqueness. First of all, we are rational beings who can make judgments and thus have moral responsibility. We have a human spirit that enables us to be indwelt by God.

Second, man is a moral being because the law of God is written on his heart. Although there may be many differences in morality among varying cultures, one common denominator is moral consciousness. Man is constantly confronted by God both in nature from without and the moral law within.

The implications are clear: No person needs to justify his right to live. Everyone, whether deformed or not, has special value. As C. S. Lewis said, there are no ordinary people. "It is immortals whom we joke with, work with, marry, snub and exploit. Immortal horrors or everlasting splendors."

(2) *A fetus is a person.*

The abortion advocates try to redefine personhood to exclude the unborn. Like Hitler, who defined personhood to exclude blacks and Jews, the abortionists try to rationalize their belief that the unborn can be killed with impunity. M. Warren suggests five traits or criteria that are essential to personhood: (1) consciousness of things external and internal to one's self, and especially the ability to feel pain; (2) reasoning; (3) self-motivated activity and activity that is independent of genetic or external controls; (4) the ability to communicate with an indefinite number of contents and topics; (5) the presence of self-concepts and awareness.[4]

With such a definition of personhood, we might question whether or not many of us would pass the test. But we can expect such redefinitions to occur as the desire to eliminate the unborn, deformed, and the elderly gains momentum.

Although the Bible was written in a day when abortion techniques had not been perfected, it speaks with clarity about the status of the unborn child. God personally fashions the fetus. "For Thou didst form my inward parts; Thou didst weave me in my mother's womb" (Psalm 139:13). Long before the discovery of the DNA code, which has enhanced our understanding of the complexity of the human body, the psalmist exulted in the wonder of God's creation. "I will give thanks to Thee, for I am fearfully and wonderfully made; wonderful are Thy works, and my soul knows it very well" (Psalm 139:14). If David had only known that his body contained thirty trillion cells and that each cell had volumes of information coded on it, he would have praised the Lord with even greater enthusiasm.

Clearly God considers the fetus as a human being. He said to Jeremiah, "Before I formed you in the womb I knew you, and before you were born I consecrated you; I have appointed you a prophet to the nations" (1:5). God is already forming plans for the unborn child whom He "knows" in advance.

Possibly the clearest indication that God regards the fetus as a person is found in comparing two verses of Scripture. In Luke 18:15 we read, "And they were

4. M. Warren, "On the Moral and Legal Status of Abortion," *Monist* 57 (1973):59.

bringing even their babies to Him, in order that He might touch them." The Greek word for baby used here is *brephos* and clearly signifies personhood. In Luke 1:41 we have the same word used when Mary, who was pregnant with Jesus, went to visit her cousin Elizabeth in the hill country of Judah. "And it came about that when Elizabeth heard Mary's greeting, the baby leaped in her womb; and Elizabeth was filled with the Holy Spirit." The fetus is called a *brephos*, a baby.

There's not a shred of evidence biblically or biologically that a fetus is just a blob of protoplasm, a "product of conception." It is interesting that many women who have had abortions later say, "I killed my baby." Many submit to an abortion only after they have been convinced that the fetus is not a person. The counsellor tells them that the unborn child is nothing but "a little collection of cells." Such terminology is used to depersonalize the baby in the mother's mind. Yet although her mind wishes to accept such neutral descriptions in order to rationalize her decision, her feelings often do not follow suite. One young woman described her abortion as being painful until it was over. Then, she said, "Mustering my strength, I called a nurse. A gentle, quiet woman assisted me, surprised that I hadn't cried out in agony. Examining the fetus she said, 'Oh look, it was a little boy.' I propped myself up and without thinking looked down at the perfectly formed little person—a boy. Hair, nails, and facial details weren't there yet, but I could see his tiny fingers and toes. This frail body smacked the reality of what I had done. He had been totally dependent upon me for life. I had killed my child."[5]

Many women, however brainwashed by contem-

5. *Moody Monthly,* May 1982, p. 43.

porary society, have later had to admit that they killed a baby. Biblically and biologically they were correct.

 (3) *To kill a fetus is to kill a person.*

Obviously, if Mary the mother of Jesus had had an abortion, Christ would not have been born in Bethlehem. If Jeremiah's mother had aborted, the prophet would not have been able to fulfill his mission.

In Exodus 21 there is a clear indication that God regards the death of a fetus to be the death of a person. Hebrew scholars both classical and modern interpret Exodus 21:22-25 to teach that if men strike a woman with child and she has a miscarriage and the child lives, the man shall be fined as the woman's husband may demand of him. But if there is any further injury (that is, if the aborted child dies) then "you shall appoint as a penalty life for life, eye for eye, tooth for tooth, hand for hand, foot for foot" (vv. 23-24). In other words, if either the unborn baby or the mother dies, there must be just retribution. *The fetus also falls under the protection of the law of retaliation.*

Nothing dramatizes the schizophrenia of our age more than the law against crushing the egg of a bald eagle. Such a person may be fined $5,000 and put in jail for one year. Incredibly, our society has adopted the notion that a baby eagle is worth more than a human being. Everyone knows that an eagle's egg is a potential eaglet subject to protection, but a fetus, we are told, is not a human being even if it should be already viable outside of the womb.

The Supreme Court used such twisted logic because it was bent on making abortion a woman's right, by hook or by crook. Those who have studied Justice Blackmun's 64-page document in detail confess that it is a mix of illogical reasoning and non sequiturs.

To illustrate, Blackmun wrote, "We need not resolve the difficult question of when life begins." Then he goes on to argue for the right to abort. Two questions come immediately to mind in one sentence of the document. (1) We do not know when life begins. Perhaps Blackmun meant *human* life, but even if that was his intention, biology assures us that the answer is that human life begins at conception. But (2) if indeed the Court cannot decide the answer as to when life begins, by what logic can it affirm that the unborn child may be killed? Harold O. J. Brown appropriately asks, What would we think of a hunter who, when he saw movement in the bushes, later reported that he was unable to resolve the difficult question of whether he saw a man or a beast and therefore decided to shoot? In other words, if the question is unresolved, shouldn't we protect life until we are sure it is not human?

"Freedom of choice" is therefore freedom to kill. One is reminded of George Orwell's *1984* where the torturers were referred to as "the ministry of love." According to Francis Schaeffer, the Nazis used the name "charitable transport company for the sick" for the agency conveying people to the killing centers.[6]

How could our justices have blundered so badly? The answer, of course, is that they bowed to the pressure of the feminists, who were calling for abortion on demand as a legitimate right. This is precisely what happened on the bench more than one hundred years earlier with the *Dred Scott* decision. This black man wanted his right to freedom, but the Supreme Court, some of whose justices themselves had slaves, chose to relegate blacks to the status of "non-persons" for personal convenience. By a seven to two vote they agreed, regarding the status of blacks, "We think that they are not included and were not intended to be

6. Francis Schaeffer, *Whatever Happened to the Human Race?* (Old Tappan, N.J.: Revell, 1979), p. 110.

included under the word citizen in the constitution and can therefore claim none of the rights and privileges which that instrument provides for and secures to the citizens of the United States."[7]

In 1973, by the same margin of seven to two the Supreme Court made a similar decision regarding the unborn.

During the sixties the new morality became openly fashionable in America. Sex with anyone anywhere as long as it was "meaningful" was accepted. The result is that there are many unwanted pregnancies. Seventy-five percent of all those who have abortions are unmarried. Abortion has become the "mopping up operation" after the devastation brought on by the breakdown of moral values.

And what about the future? Be assured that opposition to infanticide will be ridiculed as merely the opinion of a small elite that wants to impose its morality on others. Unless we stop abortion, the lives of our children and our own future as older adults will be at stake. Governor Richard Lamm from Colorado echoed the popular notion today that there is such a thing as a life not worthy to be lived when he said, "The dying have a duty to die and to get it over with."

OUR RESPONSE

Has the battle against abortion been lost? *Only if we sit by and do nothing.* Fortunately there are still political and legal options open, and as of the writing of this book, there is a ground swell of support for the prolife movement.

Everyone can do something to put an end to the violence of abortion. Public indifference must be replaced by aggressive abhorrence of these killings.

7. Dred Scott v. Sandford, 60 U.S. 393 at 404.

No person can do everything, but each of us can at least do *one* of the following.

- Write a letter to your congressman. Your letter will have greater impact if it is written courteously and at a time when a bill is pending that relates to abortion. Be assured that intelligent, well-thought-out letters are carefully considered, and it is often assumed that they represent many others with similar views.
- Public protests against abortion facilities are not only legal, but morally required if we are to stand for the value of human life. To bomb abortion clinics, however valid the motivation, is counter-productive. But picketing clinics is an effective way to draw attention to the atrocities performed behind closed doors.
- Join a prolife organization in your community. There are numerous action groups that disseminate information, give up-to-date reports, and have specific suggestions as to how you can fight abortion in your own district. Get on the mailing list of organizations such as the Christian Action Council, 422 C Street, N. E., Washington, D.C. 20002.
- Become a part of a crisis pregnancy center. It is not enough to condemn abortion, we must also stand ready to help those who are faced with the prospects of an unwanted pregnancy. In his book *The Least of These* Curt Young quotes this letter from a young woman.

I agree with you 100% on abortion, but I had one. It was the hardest thing I ever had to do in my life. My Mom said I had to have an abortion . . . The counsellor at Planned Parenthood talked to me. She said my baby would never be adopted. Who was I to turn to?

I was forbidden to see my boyfriend. My mother and father didn't want me to have the child. Now . . . would you mind telling me what *you* would have done? I didn't have a place to go, no money. Would you have taken me in to your home? Paid my doctors bills and expenses?

My abortion is something I wish I'd never done. I can remember looking at the doctor when it was done and saw him putting my baby into a plastic bag and then throwing it away in a garbage bag. Do you know how that feels? . . . Have you ever lost something you loved dearly? I did, and I'm not proud of it. If I had a place to go and people who cared about my baby and me, maybe my baby would be born alive. It was supposed to be born this month.

You're hurting girls that want their babies, but didn't have any alternative, but to have it aborted. But I want to say it hurts . . . you people are against abortion, but are you willing to help young girls and women who don't have the money or a place to live? . . . some of us women and girls are not killers. We're human too. And I can tell you that having an abortion is killing me slowly.[8]

Finally, we must repent of our hard-heartedness; our cruelty to one another. Abortion has made us callous as a nation. Almost every day a news report appears in the newspaper about child abuse. Abortion has helped spawn such crimes. Parents now reason, "If I could have killed him before he was born, why can't I do it after he is born?" If the unborn baby is garbage, birth obviously cannot bring about any sudden changes.

Meanwhile, unborn babies continue to be aborted. Twenty-six doctors have agreed that a fetus can feel pain by the time the mother knows she is pregnant. Dr.

---

8. Curt Young, *The Least of These* (Chicago: Moody, 1983), p. vii. Used by permission.

Vincent Collins, professor of anesthesiology at Northwestern University and the University of Illinois Medical Center in Chicago says that after thirty-two to thirty-six days of gestation, a developing fetus emits brain waves "almost identical to your (adult) brain waves." By forty-five days, the brain waves are identical to those of adults, he notes.

Abortion continues only because babies are not strong enough to fight back. Their cries are muffled in the sanitary surroundings of hospitals and abortion clinics. Someone has to fight their battles for them because they are helpless in the struggles. Because doctors are bigger and suction devices are stronger, the child becomes prey to those who seek to kill him. If we do not stand up for a child's rights, why do we think that our own will not be taken away? If the Christian church cannot unite in its opposition against abortion, it is highly unlikely that it can unite about anything else. Surely nothing must be more grievous to the heart of God than seeing these little ones forced into an untimely death performed under the guise of "freedom."

The following poem was written by Dr. David C. Thompson after he had witnessed an abortion.

> Tiny wonder, little human,
> Lying still, your hands outstretched.
> I wonder what you might have been.
> I wonder what you might have done.
>
> Sixteen weeks—that's all you lived
> Until they wrenched you out of the womb
> To lie unattended, gasping, stunned,
> A plastic bag to be your tomb.
>
> They weigh your form, record its length;
> Perfect tissue, soulless, mute.
> Your life, so small, was still too much.
> You died without one loving touch.

Spark of existence, now no more,
Snuffed out by those who came before.
I wonder what you might have been.
I wonder what you might have done.[9]

Can we still weep over such tiny little forms struggling
for life? The real root of the problem of abortion is
found in the human heart. With characteristic percep-
tion Jesus put His finger on the source of all human ills.
"For from within, out of the heart of men, proceed the
evil thoughts and fornications, thefts, murders, adul-
teries, deeds of coveting and wickedness, as well as
deceit, sensuality, envy, slander, pride and foolishness.
All these evil things proceed from within and defile
the man" (Mark 7:21-23). It is a wicked heart that
causes us to be unmoved by the sight of little babies
with their skin burned from the saline solution or their
bodies torn apart by a suction device.

Christ is able to take out the heart of stone and
replace it with a heart of love. Some of our most influential prolifers today are those who believed in abortion until their hearts were radically changed by Jesus Christ. Only when hardness of heart is removed
will we be able to weep with sensitivity for the atrocities of this nation.

What is more, Jesus Christ is able to cleanse those
women who have had an abortion. As one woman
told me, "Not only has Jesus Christ forgiven me, and
cleansed my conscience, but He has even taken
away the horrid, horrid memories of my abortion experience."

Christ is asking us to come to Him individually and
as a nation that the blood that stains our hands might
be washed away. Forgiveness is available for those
who respond to His love and mercy.

9. David C. Thompson, The Alliance Witness, 18 January 1984, p. 7. Used
by permission.

8

THE MYTH THAT
WE CAN IGNORE THE
GHOST OF KARL MARX

In our discussions of church-state relations we cannot ignore the one man who rules nearly one half of the world from his grave. The magnetic power of Marxism is unparalleled in history. It has captured the imagination of leaders of different continents and races, all the way from China to Russia to Cuba and Central America. It is not possible to understand what is happening in the United States today without grasping the essence of Marx's teachings.

Here in America Marx is the unseen guest at political dialogues, the shadow that hovers over the controversies discussed in this book. When the Roman Catholic bishops issue a statement that holds the American government responsible for eliminating poverty by forced taxation, government intervention, and handouts, shades of Marx are present.

When our Supreme Court refuses to recognize the existence of natural rights; when feminists insist that liberation means freedom from the burden of rearing children; and when secularists want to erect a "wall of separation" between church and state so that religion has no influence in public life, the ghost of Marx is visible.

We associate Marxism with terrorism, repression, and political enslavement. But actually, Marxism appears to many to be an attractive solution to the economic problems of the world. Liberation theology, so popular in Latin America, has attempted to combine some elements of Marxism with Christianity in an attempt to rectify the gross inequities that exist between rich and poor, the powerful and the weak.

The basic axiom of Marxism is that the poor are poor because the rich are rich. The rich are oppressors; the poor are their victims. Because the rich will not share their wealth voluntarily, the only just course is to redistribute wealth forcibly through taxation, and more important, by the state's owning all property and means of production.

That Marx has had a great influence in our society can be seen by the contempt that exists for capitalism even here in the United States. If you read the news journals you will agree with Ronald Nash, who wrote:

> Capitalism is blamed for every evil in contemporary society including its greed, materialism, and selfishness, the prevalence of fraudulent behavior, the debasement of society's tastes, the pollution of the environment, the alienation and despair within society and the vast disparities of wealth. Even racism and sexism are treated as the effects of capitalism.[1]

Given the inroads of Marxism, we can understand why some liberals believe that the United States is actually the cause of the problems in the Third World. Despite all the aid given to those countries, the blame

1. Ronald Nash, ed., *Liberation Theology* (Milford, Mich.: Mott Media, 1984), p. 50.

for the economic injustices of the world rests on the doorstep of the United States. Thanks to Marx, capitalism is believed to be the root of all evil. With such an easily identifiable cause of society's ills, some politicians naively believe that the answer is to replace our economic system with one that will rid us of the curse of capitalism and the right to private ownership. Marx believed that if private property were abolished, all prejudices and injustices would vanish. Incredibly, this myth is widely believed.

Why is Marxism so attractive? And what are its implications for human rights? And where do we see its influence in the United States? These are questions that necessitate an informed answer.

The Attraction of Marxism

Karl Marx was born to Jewish parents in the Rhineland of Germany. When Karl was six years old, his father had the whole family baptized as Lutheran Christians. Marx adopted radical ideas while studying at the University of Berlin, and he eventually went to Paris, where he met Friedrich Engels in 1844. Together they wrote the celebrated *Communist Manifesto* in 1847. Later, Marx was exiled to England where he wrote his other famous work *Das Kapital.*

England was in the throes of change caused by the Industrial Revolution. An abundance of cheap labor made it possible for the wealthy to pay low wages while maintaining poor working conditions. To Marx's credit, he was deeply concerned about the inequities that he saw in society. Women and children being forced to work, long hours, and overcrowded slums were rampant. The exploited working class was the proletariate (working class) of which he wrote.

Marx believed he had discovered the key to history and a way to bring equality to citizenry. The underpinnings of his theory are (1) materialism, the belief that matter is the final reality; there is no God, no human soul. Then (2) history follows the path of economic determinism, in other words, there are economic forces that propel history ever onward and upward. Finally, (3) Marx believed that private property was the source of all evil. When it was abolished the inequities of society would be rectified.

For Marx economics was the prime factor in history; it was the basis for exploitation, the source of laws, and the basic reason for injustice. The only way to rectify these abuses was for the proletariate to gain control of the means of production. Marx believed that history was on his side. The past was but a record of class struggles. Eventually the oppressed proletariate would overthrow the oppressors, the bourgeoisie (the ruling class). Thus history moves according to this "dialectic." Eventually a classless society would develop with complete economic justice and equality.

Man, Marx believed, could hasten this inevitable trend by participating in a revolution that would overthrow the oppressors and usher in the utopian era. This could only be brought about when private ownership, religion, and the family were all abolished, because these fostered oppression.

These ideas inspired such leaders as Mao Tse-tung of China. Faced with a country of 600 million people (in the 1930s) that was divided by independently warring states and oppressed by fuedal landlords, Marxism seemed to be the only solution to unify the country and bring about justice. Superficially at least, it makes sense to think that if the government owned all the land abuses could be abolished. Equality and economic justice could be imposed on society if the state had the authority to do so. Since the only way for this to be brought about is by a revolution, so be it. In the long run it's worth the cost.

This explains why liberation theology is so popular in Latin America. In countries such as Colombia, the capitalist government is corrupt; the poor are exploited and see no hope of economic justice. A revolution, unattractive though it may be, seems to be the only way corruption can be routed with everyone being given at least a small share of the economic pie. A young man who left the church to participate in the liberation movement put it this way, "You Protestants are anxious to make people give up smoking and drinking. The Communists are concerned about the relief of suffering and injustice."[2]

The church is thus criticized for preaching a message of individual salvation that ignores social sins. Samuel Escobar said, "We promised the neurotics that they will find spiritual peace and the psychologically disturbed that they will find the fountain of tranquillity. But what does our message have to say to the ones who exploit the Indians, to Capitalist abusers, to corrupt government officials who accept bribery, to dishonest politicians? What about the comfortable indifference in our churches toward the suffering of the masses?"[3] Thus many people who are motivated by the love of Christ in Latin America have become Marxist in hope of bringing about economic justice.

In the United States, *Sojourners* magazine, with a circulation nearing 40,000 attempts to combine Christianity with a leftist political stance. It is committed to liberation theology both for Central America and the United States. Over a period of six years it has criticized numerous countries for human rights violations, but none has been a Marxist-Leninist country. Marxist countries are always portrayed favorably, capitalistic

2. Harvie M. Conn, "The Mission of the Church," in Carl E. Amerding, ed., *Evangelicals and Liberation* (Nutley, N.J.: Presbyterian & Reformed, 1971), p. 61.
3. Ibid., p. 66.

regimes are denounced. All the while the editors claim to be expounding biblical Christianity.[4]

Clark Pinnock, an evangelical scholar who is sensitive to the plight of the poor, admits that he flirted with Marxism as a solution to the hunger and exploitation in the world. If we as humans are too selfish to share our resources with those who are starving, it might make sense to have equality brought about by the forced taxation of the rich. Along with that idea Pinnock believed that America was a Babylon that should be overthrown. This nation's exploitation contributed to the heartache of other countries. Pinnock eventually changed his mind about his involvement with liberal policies and his present testimony will enlighten interested readers.[5]

There is no doubt that Marxism is attractive as a plausible solution to the problems of the world. However, it has failed miserably because of a defective view of human nature. But before we give a critique, let's consider more carefully the views of Marx and how they have affected thinking in America today.

MARXISM AND HUMAN RIGHTS

Marx believed that law was nothing more than the expressed wish of those who held economic power. Laws were written by the dominant class for the exploitation of the poor. He declared, "Legislation, whether political or civil, never does more than proclaim, express in words, the will of economic relations."[6] Since the law originates in economics, with a change in the economy there will also be a change in

---

4. *Guidelines for Today,* November/December 1984, p. 20.
5. Ronald Nash, "A Pilgrimage in Political Theology," in Nash, pp. 105-19.
6. Karl Marx, *The Poverty of Philosophy,* p. 93. Quoted in John W. Montgomery, "The Marxist Approach to Human Rights Analysis and Critique," *The Simon Greenleaf Law Review* 3:39.

the law. Law reform will follow a reform of the economic structure. Thus after a revolution there is a change from capitalistic law to communistic law. Eventually when the utopian stage of Communism is realized, Marx believed that the law would wither away. It would be unnecessary because it, like the state, would no longer be necessary. *Law is but a means for class oppression.*

As a consequence of the belief that law is nothing more than an instrument of policy for those who rule, it follows that the end justifies the means. Lenin became weary of being told that he had no ethics because of his use of brutality. When accused of believing that the end justifies the means, he shot back, "If the end does not justify the means, then in the name of sanity and justice what does?"

Leon Trotsky in his famous dialogue with John Dewey asserted:

> A means can be justified only by its end. But the end in its turn needs to be justified. From the Marxist point of view, which expresses the historical interests of the Proletariate, the end is justified if it leads to increasing the power of man over nature and the abolition of the power of man over man . . . that is permissible . . . which *really* leads to the liberation of mankind.[7]

What are the practical implications of this belief? Lev Kopelev tells us that as a convinced Russian Marxist in the 1930s, "I firmly believed that the ends justified the means. Our great goal was the universal triumph of Communism, and for the sake of that goal everything was possible—to lie, to steal, to destroy hundreds of thousands and even millions of people,

7. Leon Trotsky, *Their Morals and Ours: Marxist Versus Liberal Views on Moralists,* quoted in Montgomery, p. 52.

all those who were hindering our work or could hinder it, everyone who stood in the way."[8] The law, then, is a means to a proper social end. It is not a fixed absolute that transcends culture, but a convenience to bring about social liberation. Laws can be made for the benefit of the state without any reference to a higher law—the end of social liberation justifies the means.

What rights do individuals have given a Marxist view of law? Remember, law is to be used as an instrument to bring about socialism. Therefore human rights do not exist as an inalienable given, but rather *the state creates whatever human rights exist.*

When the Soviet Union shot down a Korean jetliner with nearly 300 people aboard in 1983, there was an outcry from the West. Those who did not understand Marxism expressed dismay that the Soviets would kill innocent passengers riding in what was known to be an unarmed passenger plane. But such atrocities are in perfect accord with a Marxist notion that individuals have no inherent rights, only those conferred by the state. Those who stand in the way of the state's goals can be legally eliminated. Human rights can be either conferred or retracted as the state sees fit.

Recent events in Poland have been embarrassing to the Communist regime. Since Communism prides itself in taking the side of the working class one might think that the right to strike would be a fundamental "workers' right," but it is not. Nothing, not even the collective will of the oppressed, is allowed to threaten state authority. As Rene David emphasized, "Soviet leaders are placed above the law by Marxist doctrine itself, for law is considered simply as a means at their dis-

---

8. Lev Kopelev, *No Jail for Thought,* pp. 31-34. Quoted in Montgomery, p. 139.

posal, not as an absolute value dictating their conduct."[9]

As Montgomery has pointed out, if the state is regarded as the sole source of human rights, it follows that one cannot logically criticize the state for human rights violations. "Without the state human rights would be nonexistent, so to criticize her is tantamount to biting the hand that feeds you."[10]

Clearly the ghost of Marx was present when the Supreme Court gave women an absolute right to an abortion without any interference by the father or grandparents of the child. The *Roe* v. *Wade* argument is that "the state has no compelling interest in the life of the unborn." Notice that abortion was legalized because the *state* saw no reason to protect the life of the unborn. Whether the child had any natural rights, whether the father or the grandparents wanted the child, was not determinative. Only the interests of the state mattered.

Notice the logic: because the unborn is not of sufficient value to the state, the state has no interest in or right to protect it. As Harold O. J. Brown says, "This is a total reversal of fundamental American values: the rights of individuals do not come from their value to the state, but from the Creator."[11] Brown continues by saying that it does not take much imagination to see where the doctrine of "compelling state interest" will lead us when bureaucrats begin to add up the cost of caring for the old, the handicapped, the retired, and even those who are underproducers.

And where does this notion of human rights eventu-

9. René David and J. Brierley, *Major Legal Systems in the World Today,* p. 158. Quoted in Montgomery, p. 102.
10. Montgomery, p. 79.
11. Harold O. J. Brown, *Death Before Birth* (Nashville: Thomas Nelson, 1977), p. 92.

ally lead? Pressure is beginning to build to take the next logical step. A good example is China, where abortion was initially voluntary, but now is government policy. Each couple is permitted only one child. If the woman becomes pregnant a second time, the baby is aborted. Even women in their last months of pregnancy are rounded up, herded onto trucks, and taken to hospitals so abortions may be performed. Read carefully the words of Qian Xinzhong the Minister of Family Planning, "Births are a matter of state planning, just like other economic and social activities, because they are a matter of strategic concern . . . a couple cannot have a baby just because it wants to."[12]

According to the Christian Action Council, the United States has in the past helped fund China's abortion program through its large grants to the International Planned Parenthood Federation and the United Nations Fund for Population Activities. I might add that in 1983 the United Nations gave a family-planning award to India and China.

All of this helps us to understand the real intentions of the abortion movement in the United States. As we make the transition from a Judeo-Christian understanding to secularism, abortion is for now voluntary. But when human rights are fully in the hands of the state, there is no telling where the line will be drawn. Forced abortions in the United States could be required unless there is a return to the belief that man is endowed by his Creator with certain inalienable rights.

The bottom line, of course, is that in Marxism the state is everything, the individual is nothing. The state owns the people that live in it. Any laws can be

12. *Chicago Sun-Times*, 18 February 1985, p. 6.

passed to further the state's interest. Gone is the notion that individuals have inherent rights.

We should notice in passing that Marx believed that eventually his theory of economics and human rights would become global. He believed that Marxism with its belief in the forced redistribution of wealth, the elimination of religious values, and establishment of a socialist world order would triumph. Interestingly the *Humanist Manifesto* shares similar objectives. "Thus we look to the development of a system of world law and a world order based on transnational federal government . . . world poverty must cease. Hence extreme disproportions in wealth, income, and economic growth should be reduced on a world wide basis."[13] Though no specifics are given as to how this could be achieved, Marxism with its emphasis on state control is an attractive solution to the secular mind.

MARXISM, RELIGION, AND THE FAMILY

Marx, you will recall, believed that religion was the opiate of the people. He agreed with Feuerbach that "all religion . . . is nothing but the fantastic reflection in men's minds of those external forces which control their daily life, a reflection in which the terrestrial forces assume the form of supernatural forces."[14] Religion was invented for the purpose of repression; it was one more scheme of capitalism to oppress the poor. Marx taught that religion must be forcibly abolished.

There is evidence that Marx was not so much an

13. Paul Kurtz, ed., *Humanist Manifestos I and II* (New York: Prometheus, 1973), p. 21.
14. Reinhold Niebuhr, ed., *Marx and Engels on Religion* (New York: Schocken, 1964), p. 147.

atheist as a man who hated the God in whom he believed. He wanted to ruin the world and thereby show his own equality with God. In his poem *Human Pride* he wrote:

> With disdain I will throw my gauntlet
> Full in the face of the world,
> And see the collapse of this pygmy giant
> Whose fall will not stifle my ardour.
>
> Then will I wander godlike and victorious
> Through the ruins of the world
> And, giving my words an active force,
> I will feel equal to the creator.[15]

If Marx is the messiah of Communism, Lenin is its apostle Paul. He wrote, in a letter to Maksim Gorki in 1913, "Millions of sins, filthy deeds, acts of violence and physical epidemics, are far less dangerous than the subtle spiritual idea of God."

In the *Communist Manifesto,* Marx answers the objections some will raise about the abolition of the family. He responds, "On what foundation is the present family, the bourgeoisie family based? On Capital, on private gain. In its completely developed form this family exists only among the bourgeoisie . . . the bourgeoisie family will vanish as a matter of course when its complement vanishes, and both will vanish with the vanishing of capital."[16]

Of course children, like all subjects in a Marxist country, belong to the state. Therefore the state has the responsibility of educating them and bringing them

15. Karl Marx and Friedrich Engels, *Historisch-kritisch Gesamtausgabe. Werke, Schriften, Briefe,* ed. David Rajazanov (Frankfurt: Marx-Engels Archiv, 1927), sec. 1, vol. 1, pt. 2, p. 50. Cited in Richard Wurmbrand, *Was Karl Marx a Satanist?* (Glendale, Calif.: Diane Books, 1976), p. 25.
16. Marx and Engels, "Manifesto of the Communist Party," in Lewis S. Feuer, ed., *Marx and Engels* (New York: Anchor, 1959), p. 24.

up with the religion of Marxism. Along with this is the liberation of women. The socialist woman is not one who is expected to rear children, but she can directly participate in economic production. In fact, her value is intimately linked to productivity. *To work outside the home is to become a valuable member of society.*

This explains why the radical feminists in this country derive much of their vision from the literature of socialism. In fact, they admit that their goals cannot be achieved in a capitalistic society. As Lenin put it, "We cannot be free if one-half the population is enslaved in the kitchen." Nor can a country be free if parents have the right to teach their children religion.

THE CHURCH AND STATE

With the rise of groups such as the Moral Majority, the separation of church and state has received much attention. As long as liberals dominated politics, no one raised the issue. But when conservatives became active we heard a chorus of objections shouting that there was a "wall of separation" between church and state. As we all know, the phrase does not appear in the United States Constitution but in a letter written by Thomas Jefferson.

What is important to remember is that Marxist states believe in a wall of separation between church and state. For example, the Soviet Constitution provides:

> Article 124.
> In order to ensure to citizens freedom of conscience, the church in the U.S.S.R. is separated from the state and the school from the church. Freedom of religious worship and freedom of anti-religious propaganda is recognized for all citizens.

In Communist countries religion is free to operate in those areas where the state does not have control. But because the state controls virtually all areas of its citizens' lives, religion is effectively abolished.

Although the secularists in America do not categorically state that they want to abolish religion, they do want to confine its influence so that it in no way affects public policy. A good illustration of this mind-set was a speech given by Governor Mario Cuomo of New York in 1984, who said that although he was personally opposed to abortion, he would never dream of imposing his values on society, *nor would he allow his views to influence public policy.* In other words, his Christianity was a belief that could be confined only to his mind, but it would in no way influence his life.

In Marxist countries the leaders admit that they cannot stop religion—in other words, they cannot control what people think. But they can make sure that religion does not influence the way people live. *In other words, it's permissible to have Christian ideas as long as these in no way spill over to your life-style.* This is a new understanding of the separation of church and state that is being heralded in America.

Marxists redefine human rights to suit the aims of the socialist state. Freedom of speech means that you are permitted to say anything that is not detrimental to the state. Freedom of religion means that you can think whatever you like, just as long as it does not influence the way you live. Freedom in education means that anything can be taught as long as it is approved by the state. All meaningful words are bleached from their usual connotations and given a Marxist twist.

A CRITIQUE

Although no one doubts the importance of economic factors, in making economics the dominant factor in the movement of history, Marx was mistaken. To think that the ownership of private property is the root of all evil is, to say the least, naive. History must also be explained by political, educational, and religious considerations. No one factor is the source of all the rest.

Even more serious is Marx's fatal misunderstanding of human nature. He actually believed that if the proletariate took over, a classless society would eventually emerge that would end all exploitation. Although he believed that capitalists exploited the poor, manipulated economic systems to suit their own ends, human nature would suddenly become selfless and caring once a suitable economic environment is provided. In fact, human beings under these conditions would spontaneously act lawfully and eventually both the state and the law would wither away.

Marx's error was to believe that man's difficulties are no more than the product of external social conditions. As John Warwick Montgomery points out, "Man himself created the conditions of exploitation—and therefore what kind of logic justifies the belief that by removing those conditions man will suddenly be rendered incapable of recapitulating them? The root difficulty lies not with the 'economy' (or with any other impersonal factor); it lies in the heart of man himself."[17]

Clearly Karl Marx misjudged human nature.

Thus as we return to the problems in Latin America, or the ruling of our Supreme Court, and the feminist movement, we find the ghost of Marx has traveled with us. But at root his theory has a defective view of human nature. Marxism can at best replace one corrupt regime for another. The violations of human dignity that occur in a Marxist understanding of law are too numerous to document. But for starters we can

17. Montgomery, p. 169.

read a book such as *The Gulag Archipelago* by Aleksandr Solzhenitsyn. Meanwhile, no state seems to be in the process of withering away, and no classless society has yet emerged.

As emphasized, by believing that man's value depends upon his productivity and that he exists solely for the state, the Marxist can assign no real value to personhood. To think that man could usher in a utopia if only he were presented with the correct economic conditions is absurd.

As Pinnock, who was at one time enamored with Marxism, wrote, "We radicals thought we loved peace and justice, but we simply did not grasp the nature of tyranny in the modern world."[18] He adds, "I have come to feel with so many others that socialism represents a false prophecy and cruel delusion. It is an enemy of the poor because it destroys prosperity. By uniting economic and political power in one center, it produces tyranny. Marxism promised to explain and change the world but it has done neither."[19]

If we wish to understand man's problems and a solution in the correct light, we must return to the Scriptures.

THE RESPONSE OF THE CHURCH

That the Marxist solution to economic injustice is a failure, there can be little doubt. But some of the blame for its continuing attractiveness rests with the church, which has often been indifferent to the needs of the poor. Because of our emphasis on saving souls, we have frequently neglected man's physical body. For such failure, we are indicted. Though there is no question but that man's ultimate problem is spiritual and therefore the gospel must be preached to

18. Clark Pinnock, "A Pilgrimage in Political Theology," in Nash, p. 112.
19. Ibid., p. 117.

change the human heart, we have often been defective in showing the application of the gospel to the concrete hardships of life.

Consider for example the retreat of the church from the inner cities of our nation. As a whole, evangelical Christianity has not wanted to be bothered by the plight of those in the ghetto. As someone has said, the average American passes by the poor on the road of life without a twinge of conscience. He feels he has paid the Good Samaritan to come and take care of this unpleasant social obligation. Uncle Sam will give the economically wounded a handout, and thus relieve us of any personal obligation.

The failure of the welfare system in the United States is well documented in John Perkin's book *With Justice for All*.[20] There he vividly portrays the plight of the black community with its hopelessness and despair. But rather than aiding the poor, the welfare system has split families, created dependency, and actually killed the ambition of those who benefit from it.

What is the answer? Perkins has developed a community approach to the problem. It can be summarized by the three R's. The first is *Relocation*. If the church is serious in helping the poor, it must live in their neighborhoods. However much we might want to help by remote control, we simply cannot do so by isolating ourselves from human need. Believers must return to the cities and live alongside those who are the victims of economic and social problems. Handouts will not do. Paying someone else to play the part of the Good Samaritan cannot alleviate us of personal responsibility.

Then there is *Reconciliation*. We must get acquainted with those who simply do not have the same op-

20. John Perkins, *With Justice for All* (Glendale, Calif.: Regal, 1982). This book deserves to be read by every thoughtful Christian. It exposes the need in our nation's cities, but also gives a realistic plan for action.

portunities as we. So many barriers exist between the ethnic groups in our society that bridges must be built, friendships begun. How else can the church that claims to have Christ's love demonstrate its own authenticity but by such involvement? To *say* that we have love, and then turn away from the cries of those around us is a denial of the gospel's power.

The next step is *Redistribution.* That is a willingness to share resources—not just money, but the creative resources of the church with those in need.

Dozens of examples could be given of churches that have worked with the poor in installing wood-burning stoves to conserve fuel, the distributing of clothes, and giving counsel and dental care. The opportunities are endless, the rewards great.

But are we willing to pay the price? Or will we continue to talk about the problem and then retreat back into our life of personal affluence and prosperity? Marxism should be a challenge to the church. It is not enough to counteract it intellectually—we have to disprove the false notion that the rich must be rich at the expense of the poor. As Francis Schaeffer put it, we must have "capitalism with compassion." There's no doubt that capitalism has often exploited the poor and appealed to the greed of the human heart. But within the Christian community at least, the love and sacrificial involvement of believers should be an attractive alternative to the false hopes of the utopian dream.

There is a story of a church in Germany that was destroyed during World War II. As the rubble was cleared away, a statue of Christ was found with the hands missing. Apparently a famous sculptor offered to restore the hands, but the officers of the church declined, saying that this was a symbol of our Lord's dependence on the hands of His followers to serve Him in the loving concern and compassion for others.

Marxism should not be faulted because of its desire in bringing about economic justice. Indeed, we must commend Marx for bringing economics to the forefront of the thinking of the world. Unfortunately, his answer was misguided. But it is up to us to prove to the world that human beings need not be *forced* to share their wealth, but with a change of heart wrought by the power of the gospel, they can do so because they delight in economic justice. Thus the ghost of Marxism in our society should not only be a cause for alarm, but also a challenge to prove that there is a relationship between Christianity and economics. The ghost won't leave until we're prepared to prove that there is a better way.

9

THE MYTH THAT PORNOGRAPHY IS A HARMLESS ADULT PLEASURE

America's obsession with pornography was national news when Miss America of 1983 appeared nude in *Penthouse* magazine. Sales of the obscene publication escalated by several million when the news broke that Miss America had been photographed in explicit lesbian poses.

What caused sales of the magazine to skyrocket? After all, pornographic magazines had shown similar scenes of other equally provocative women. But this was different. Here was a woman who was representing a pageant that, at least outwardly, had an image of moral virtue. Yet she too had been trapped into the lucrative porn market. Pornography was given new respectability; even a Miss America could appear unclad for all to see.

Is pornography a harmless pleasure? The report of the President's Commission on Obscenity and Pornography, published in 1971, concluded that the use of pornography was not harmful to society. To quote from its conclusion, "Can it be said, in the face of the evidence, that pornography is harmful to the consumers, leading them to the bottom of society and to personal misery? Here the answer must be no."[1]

Was the report accurate? The reseachers tried to find out whether there was a direct correlation between a specific crime and the use of pornography. If a rape occurred, did it happen because the criminal was influenced by pornographic materials? If such a link could not be established, then pornography was considered unrelated to the act.

In a minority report, commission member Charles H. Keating, Jr. produced extensive documentation that in some cases, enough to be statistically significant, pornography does indeed cause crime. He cited twenty-six cases, drawn from all over the country, where immersion in pornography immediately preceded serious sex crimes, many of which were admitted by the perpetrators to be enactments of pornography that was absorbed shortly before. For example: Seven Oklahoma teenage male youths gang-attacked a fifteen-year-old female from Texas, raping her and forcing her to commit unnatural acts with them. Four of the youths admitted to being incited to commit the act by reading obscene magazines and looking at lewd photographs.[2]

Aside from those specific correlations, what was also omitted from the President's Commission on Obscenity and Pornography was the more general cause-effect relationship between pornography and crime, perversion and sexual abuse. Although it is not always possible to show a one-to-one correspondence between a sex crime and pornography, the

1. *Technical Report of the Commission on Obscenity and Pornography,* vol. IX (Washington: U.S. Government Printing Office, n.d.), p. 467.
2. "The Black Plague of Pornography." Statement of Charles H. Keating, Jr., to the U.S. Senate Judiciary Committee.

fact that pornography disposes one to such acts cannot be denied.

Young people have confessed to me that pornography gave them such powerful fantasies that they would walk down the street looking for a sex partner—anyone who was available. Pornography pushed them into relationships when they were not emotionally ready, often damaging their chances for a satisfying sex life within marriage. Because the first sexual experience has such enormous importance in setting the tone for an adult's sexuality, thousands of couples can trace the seeds of marital strife to relationships that had subtle but lasting psychological consequences. Often pornography stimulated such relationships.

Our nation is drowning in a sea of sensuality. With explicit magazines, sensual movies, and video tapes readily available, we are rotting from the inside. Though pornography promises like a god, it pays like the devil. It gives the message that sex is for pleasure only and to be divorced from all responsibility. What is the message that pornography gives to this nation?

AN EXAGGERATED VIEW OF SEXUALITY

In pornography, nudity is exploited for purely erotic reasons. But when one level of stimuli loses its appeal, the victim of pornography must graduate to the next level of indecency. So he moves on to unnatural expressions of sexuality such as sadomasochism and other perversions. On and on the hapless subject is driven by an endless quest for new sexual experiences. But satisfaction is as elusive as ever. As the writer of Proverbs wrote so accurately, "Sheol and Abaddon are never satisfied, nor are the eyes of man ever satisfied" (Proverbs 27:20).

Those who are addicted to pornography soon find that the normal relationship between a man and a woman in marriage loses its appeal. The only way the marriage can be sustained, if at all, is through bizarre forms of sexuality, often against the objection of one of the partners. Even then one must move on to multiple sexual partners to continue the wild goose chase that inevitably ends in the wilderness of guilt, frustration, and emptiness. As John Drakeford wrote in an article entitled "The Sexual Mirage," pornography has "strained the traditional relationship between husband and wife. Pornography presents an unreal view of human sexuality. It is an exaggerated, fantasized view. If a husband or wife see this perspective as the norm, it is going to do a great deal of damage to the sexual relationship."[3] One half of all divorces take place because of adultery; often the adultery was encouraged by pornography.

As Nicholas von Hoffman, a *Washington Post* columnist put it:

Why is it liberals who believe "role models" in third grade readers are of decisive influence on behavior when it concerns racism or male chauvinist piggery, laugh at the assertion that pornography may also teach rape? Every text book in every public school system in the nation has been overhauled in the last 20 years because it was thought that the blond, blue-eyed suburban children once depicted therein taught little people a socially dangerous ethnocentrism. If text books, those vapid and insipid instruments of such slight influence, can have had such a sweeping effect, what are we to surmise about the effects on the impressionably young of an R- or an X-rated movie, in wide

3. John Drakeford, "The Sexual Mirage," *United Evangelical Action,* July/August 1984, p. 4.

screen technicolor, with Dolby sound and every device of cinematic realism?[4]

Charles H. Keating, Jr., in his report to the Senate Judiciary Committee, reports that a recent study done by the Michigan State Police, using a computer to classify over 35,000 sex crimes committed in that state alone over a twenty-year period, found that 43 percent were pornography-related. These are the cases in which the perpetrator was apprehended. Keating goes on to say that no one knows how many cases of sexual assault, lewd conduct, voyeurism, quasi-consensual perversion, bestiality, rape-murder, and other crimes for which the perpetrator was never caught were motivated by pornographic immersion. In those cases the authorities could never obtain the materials that triggered his sick conduct.[5]

Pornography gives a distorted view of human sexuality. It stresses the erotic without so much as giving a hint as to where its path will lead. It suggests endless pleasure without guilt, venereal disease, pregnancy, or criminal activity.

PORNOGRAPHY AND SEXUAL ABUSE

According to news reports, one out of four children will, in all likelihood, be abused by adults who themselves were abused as children. The consequences are frightening. If the cycle is not broken, the number of emotional misfits will be staggering. The more children of one generation who are sexually abused, the greater the number of potential child abusers there will be in the next generation. An abused child grows

4. Quoted by Tom Minnery, "What It Takes to Fight Pornography," *Christianity Today,* 15 February 1985, p. 11.
5. Keating, "Black Plague of Pornography."

up thinking that an adult can do whatever he likes with a child and get away with it. But not all child abusers have a history of abuse in their own childhood. Pornography in general and child pornography in particular break down a person's resistance to child abuse. What you read and fantasize about today, you *will do* tomorrow. What the mind sees and the body feels will eventually be acted out. All that is necessary is a suitable opportunity.

FBI Agent Kenneth V. Lanning told a special Senate subcommittee in 1984 that pornography helps child molesters justify their actions and trains children to accept the abuse. He testified that hundreds of thousands of pedophiles—people with a desire for sexual intercourse with children—live in the United States. Almost always they collect child pornography. This material, Lanning said, fuels their fantasies, and they use it to lower the inhibitions of children.[6]

Incest victim Katherine Brady told the same subcommittee that "Pornography trained me to respond to my father's sexual demands . . . it frightened and confused me and yet excited me and I felt trapped. My only means of surviving psychologically was to become detached, to send my mind off to pretend that the abuse was happening to someone else."[7]

A police vice squad reported that 77 percent of those who molest boys and 87 percent of those who molest girls admitted to emulating the sexual behavior found in pornography. In one group of rapists 57 percent indicated they acted out the kind of behavior they had seen in erotic material.[8]

Because there are more than two hundred monthly magazines catering to pedophiles, we can understand why the sexual abuse of children is on the in-

6. *Chicago Sun-Times,* 9 August 1984, p. 4.
7. Ibid.
8. Ibid.

crease. As long as our society is willing to tolerate pornography we can expect sexual abuse to continue.

THE DEADENING OF THE CONSCIENCE

Even the most defiled person experiences a sense of shame while staring lustfully at pornographic pictures. Though the use of pornography is by no means limited to men, women have often been the most sorely exploited. As Drakeford puts it, "Has a woman no more value than to stimulate male sexuality? Isn't she indeed an intelligent human being capable of making her own decisions? But pornography makes her simply a mindless play thing for men."[9]

Kenneth Kantzer, writing in *Christianity Today,* asserts, "But the morally sensitive person recognizes that in the long run pornography is more devastating to society than theft. Stealing robs us of things; pornography robs us of character. Stealing destroys property; pornography destroys our humanity."[10]

A person caught in the web of pornography knows its debilitating effects, but is driven by an appetite for more pornography that grows stronger as it is fed. He keeps violating his conscience, trying desperately to rationalize his foul habits. He is driven to override his own inner moral sensitivity. His conscience becomes hardened so he more easily tolerates dishonesty, laziness, and moral degeneracy in general. Because he abuses people in his mind, he will find it easier to abuse them physically later on.

When a person begins the journey into the world of pornography he has no control over his destination. The end result is out of his own hands. As Christ

9. Drakeford, p. 6.
10. Kenneth Kantzer, "Policing Pornography for Christians Who Care," *Christianity Today,* 27 June 1980, p. 10.

warned, "Truly truly, I say to you, every one who com-
mits sin is the slave of sin" (John 8:34). It is not up to the
slave to determine what he can or cannot do. That is
the decision of the master. Once we give ourselves to
sin we no longer play by *our* rules but by the ruthless
whim of a wicked being who is much more powerful
than we.

Listen to one's man story of where pornography
eventually led him:

> I was married at 19 to a nice girl. She was three months
> pregnant at the time as I had exercised my learned
> behavior and forced her into engaging sexually while
> petting. After we were married I continued to experi-
> ment sexually both in marriage and in extramarital
> affairs. The pornographic literature continued to goad
> me into the "ultimate experience." Of course that is a lie
> and has captured many young people. While married
> I seduced several women . . . I even had an affair with
> our 13-year old baby-sitter . . . I would show her pic-
> tures of young girls posing nude to encourage her to
> be more free with herself toward me . . . eventually I
> left my wife and children to pursue the "happiness" I
> thought I needed and had been programmed to look
> for.[11]

The man's story does not end there. Of course, it
never does. His dream did not come to pass but end-
ed with another divorce. Meanwhile as his children
have grown up and learned of their father's life-style,
it has damaged their respect and relationship with
him. Fortunately, God finally got his attention. Later he
surrendered himself to Christ, but the scars of pornography remain. He ends by saying, "All of this suffering
because of my reading pornography! I wish that I'd
been blind—then I'd never seen it."[12]

11. *National Federation of Decency Journal*, July/August 1984, p. 3.
12. Ibid.

No one can calculate the number of divorces, the emotional scars, the bondage, and the guilt that pornography has brought to America. Only a massive effort on the part of thousands of people can possibly stem the rush to judgment that this plague has brought.

Can anything be done?

THE ROLE OF THE LAW

The very mention of the word *law* in connection with pornography raises a chorus of objections: Censorship! Narrowmindedness! Puritanism! That such a response comes to the minds of many is a sad commentary on our day. To think that our children in public schools cannot sing Christmas carols under the guise of violating the first amendment, and yet pornographers can have freedom of speech.

But the first amendment has always been understood to have certain limitations. Even Justice Burger said, "To equate the free and robust exchange of ideas and political debate with the commercial exploitation of obscene material . . . demeans the first amendment and its purposes in the historical struggle for freedom."[13]

The debate regarding censorship involves a long-standing clash between public morality versus individual liberty. Conservatives argue that individual liberty must be curtailed when the exploitation of children, the degrading of women, and the disintegration of society is at stake. Libertarians think that any restriction of expression violates the first amendment. But the Constitution has always had some restrictions on freedom of speech and the press. Laws forbid incitement to violence, libel, slander, fraudulent adver-

13. Quoted in Reo Christenson, "It's Time to Excise the Pornographic Cancer," *Christianity Today*, 2 January 1981, p. 21.

tising, and so forth. As one writer puts it, "Wise laws against pornography do not inhibit the freedom to express ideas; they restrict profiteering aimed at the destruction of society."[14] In a free society there is a delicate balance between individual liberty and the collective good. Though we may disagree as to where the line should be drawn, it is foolish to suggest that the pendulum must favor only one side of the equation. As Christianson says, "We have had obscenity laws throughout our history and they have never lead to a creeping repression of press freedom. There is not a shred of empirical evidence to support the notion that censorship of obscenity threatens free expression of heretical political, social or religious ideas. What sensible person really believes that if we enforce the antipornographic laws we would start censoring the *New York Times?*"[15]

The argument is often made that pornography is difficult to define, hence it cannot be prosecuted by law. But to quote Christianson again, "If obscenity is impossible to define, why do opponents of censorship concede that society can legitimately protect children from it? If we can't define it, what do we keep from our kids?"[16] And I might add, why are certain cable television programs shown in the late night hours so that children are unlikely to view them? If pornography cannot be defined, how do the programmers know what to show after midnight?

The ordinary person knows that pornography cheapens and demeans. If enough citizens complain to local prosecutors, the laws that are already on the books could be applied in court. We are thankful for organizations such as the National Federation for Decency that wage the battle against pornography.

14. Kantzer, p. 11.
15. Christenson, p. 23.
16. Ibid., p. 21.

Some important gains have been made. There are cities in the United States where adult book shops have been closed all because of the insistence of citizens that the laws be applied. Millions of decent citizens could, if they wished, boycott those stores where pornography is sold. And once our impact is felt, pornography could be severely restricted. Christianson believes that the attorney general of the United States should receive "a blizzard of mail requesting the enforcement of the federal law that prohibits obscene materials from moving in interstate commerce. Wave after wave of local prosecutions in every state along with prosecutions in federal district courts, could deal the pornographers the staggering blow they so richly deserve—and which social responsibility requires."[17]

PORNOGRAPHY AND THE CHURCH

A generation ago we heard sermons against attending movies. The arguments were (1) that participating in such entertainment helps fund Hollywood, and (2) that what was shown was not biblical morality but the perversions of the world. Committed Christians simply had no time for such worldliness.

But the mood has changed. Members of the current generation claim to be better educated than their forefathers; more sophisticated, more liberated. They understand that the theater is actually neutral—it can be used for either good or evil. So this generation has begun to select what movies it will see. Hollywood has helped by producing *The Sound of Music* and other family films. Theater attendance is now acceptable in much of the evangelical community.

But it is difficult to draw the line. So Christians have begun to attend movies that are more risque. They

17. Ibid., p. 23.

often comment, "The movie was great . . . if only one
or two of the scenes would have been cut." So nudity
and violence are tolerated. Because of the explosive
power of sexuality, that invisible line has been pushed
further and further down the path of sensuality. Young
people particularly were bound to find ways to see
sexually provocative movies and once their appetite
was whetted, they became addicted.

Now with the video explosion everything is up for
grabs. Christians who would not have been seen within a hundred yards of a theater now can watch R-
rated movies in the privacy of their own living rooms.
Young people whose parents are busy making money
have become dissatisfied with materialism and have
turned toward sensual living. All of the fears that our
forefathers once had have come to pass. The church
itself is now the victim of sensuality.

What is our assignment as leaders within the
church? *Nothing less than reclaiming the moral environment in which our families and children live.* Giv-
en the proliferation of pornography in the media, the
popularity of explicit and immoral music, and the
wide-scale acceptance of divorce and immorality,
this is a formidable task indeed.

Can we even seriously think of winning? The faint-
hearted may be tempted to retreat from the battle, to
refuse active duty on the grounds that the best we can
do is to make sure that we ourselves are kept unspot-
ted from the world. They would say that the best we
can do is to prepare for the final triumph of evil.

But if we are serious about cleaning up our act,
where do we begin? Peter exhorts us, "Beloved, I urge
you as aliens and strangers to abstain from fleshly
lusts, which wage war against the soul" (1 Peter 2:11).
To influence our world we must commit ourselves to
three propositions.

1. *We are different from the world.* Peter uses the description of aliens and strangers. An alien or foreigner is one who is not familiar with his surroundings and does not feel at home. He is uncomfortable with the manners and customs of the people with whom he lives. As Christians we often do not behave as foreigners. We feel quite at home, having absorbed the culture of our society. Just think of what would happen if we were to commit ourselves anew to purity, a dogged determination not to be defiled with the world. It might mean getting rid of our television set, video recorders, and certainly any reading material that leads us into sensuality. If purity and power are related as the Bible teaches they are, think of the blessing that would come to the church if we would cut out the leaven wherever it is found.

2. *We are at war with the world.* Peter says that sinful lusts *war against the soul.* The Greek word means "a military campaign." The devil and the world have declared war against the Christian. However neutral you might want to be in the conflict, you are involved. The world is so hostile toward God that even to love it is to be God's enemy.

In some wars the outcome is genuinely in doubt; some days it looks as if side A will win, the next week the odds favor side B. But in our battle with sensuality, the scales have tilted so far that parity has been lost long ago. Our nation is drowning in a sea of sensuality, and we are being taken along with it. And what is at stake in the battle? Nothing less than total domination. Satan, through sensuality, wants to ruin our homes and thus ruin our children. He is not interested in a compromise; he is concerned that we bow in allegiance to the gods of this world.

No Christian is neutral in the conflict. The real question is whether we are willing to do whatever God may require to win the battle. The stakes are high, and the battle intense.

3. *We are watched by the world.* Peter continues by saying that we should keep our behavior excellent among the Gentiles, "so that in the thing in which they slander you as evil doers, they may on account of your good deeds, as they observe them, glorify God in the day of visitation" (1 Peter 2:12). If we do not maintain our purity as a church, what do we have to say to the world? If it is true that there are as many divorces within the church as there are outside of it; if our young people see the same movies as the young people of the world, we have just sold our influence. The early Romans were impressed with the Christians because of the visible purity of the church in the midst of paganism. Unfortunately, I don't believe the world is smitten with conviction when it sees today's church.

Can pornography destroy America? Yes. As Edmund Burke wrote when speaking of Britain, "Men are qualified for civil liberty in exact proportion to their disposition to moral chains upon their own appetites . . . society cannot exist unless a controlling power upon will and appetite be placed somewhere; and the less of it there is within, the more there is without. It is ordained in the eternal constitution of things that men of intemperate minds cannot be free."[18]

Only the people of God can arrest our society's slide into the cesspool of sensuality. But the question is

18. Quoted in David Jeremiah, *Before It's Too Late* (Nashville: Thomas Nelson, 1982), p. 74.

whether we have the moral fiber to put our own house in order so that we can speak to the world.

May God help us to take back the moral environment in which our families and children live. If not, we invite the judgment of God.

10

THE MYTH THAT
THE CHURCH SHOULD HAVE
NO VOICE IN GOVERNMENT

"**R**ender to Caesar the things that are Caesar's, and to God the things that are God's" (Mark 12:17).

This statement of Christ's was revolutionary. To those believers who were under the Roman yoke He said that we can, under certain conditions, have loyalty both to God and to the state. But Christ also knew that conflict between the two spheres would become inevitable when the secular authority would demand for himself honors that belong only to God. Yet, as far as possible, believers should live with loyalty to both authorities.

Church-state conflict goes back to the early days when Christianity was outlawed and was set in opposition to Roman rule. Early Christians died not because the Romans were intolerant (they would accept whatever god anyone wished to worship). What they abhorred was the *exclusivism* of Christianity. The belief that Jesus Christ was the *only* Lord galled the Romans and led many Christians to the lions.

Early Christianity was a minority religion in a secular state. But all of that changed under Constantine, who wanted to make Christianity coextensive with the state. In other words, everyone who would be born within the boundaries of the Roman Empire would be a Christian.

As a result of this development, the church and state were united. In the eleventh century, Pope Gregory VII struggled with the mightiest king in Western Europe, Henry IV of Germany. The question was, Who would have the authority to appoint bishops? The king insisted that that was his prerogative, but the pope maintained that such a conclusion would place the church subordinate to the state and hence corrupt the faith. When King Henry visited the pope's castle in Italy, he was required to stand barefoot for three days and ask for mercy before receiving the pope's pardon. It made sense to the pontiff that the church should have authority over the state so that heretics could be punished and doctrinal purity maintained.

Later when the Anabaptists revolted against the unity of church and state, they were put to death and persecuted with the full approval of the Reformers. Men such as Luther believed that if the church were considered to be a segment of society rather than coextensive with society, the social order would be broken up. The Anabaptists who held the strict separation of church and state were therefore persecuted for their belief.

When the Pilgrims came to what today is called the United States it was to escape the tyranny of a state church. They understood that when church and state were united there was not only a loss of individual freedom but the abuse of using civil power to enforce the whim of the religious elite.

In our Constitution these familiar words appear: "Congress shall make no law respecting an establishment of religion, or prohibiting the free exercise thereof." Clearly the intention was (1) to limit the power of the federal government by ensuring that it would not establish a state church, then (2) it was not to prohibit the free exercise of religion.

Today this amendment is being deliberately misinterpreted to try to separate God from government. Whenever any religious influence is exerted in government agencies, the secularists cry "Foul!" And if a citizen raises his voice against secularism he is told to be silent because of the supposed "wall of separation" between church and state.

The phrase "wall of separation" does not appear in the Constitution, but had its origin in a letter written by Thomas Jefferson in 1802 to a group of Baptists and Congregationalists in Danbury, Connecticut who had called him an infidel. He then said there should be a "wall of separation between church and state."

Interestingly, the USSR constitution *does* use the expression "wall of separation between church and state." This basic tenet is found in most Communist countries. Churches are permitted to operate in all those areas where the political authorities do not have power, but because the state has supreme authority over all matters, religion is literally squeezed out of existence.

The fathers of this nation never dreamed that separation of church and state meant that God should be separated from government. The government buildings in Washington bear ample testimony to the belief that faith in God is the basis for establishing laws and running the affairs of a nation.

For example, the Ten Commandments hang over the head of the chief justice of the Supreme Court (would that they had been read before the infamous *Roe* v. *Wade* decision of 1973). In the rotunda the words "In God we trust" are engraved, and on the Library of Congress we have "The heavens declare the glory of God and the firmament showeth His handiwork." The Washington monument and other government buildings contain phrases of Scripture.

The Bible has much to say about the Christian's responsibility in government.

SUPPLICATION

Most letters that congressmen receive are complaints from their constituents. Seldom are they ever affirmed and told that they are doing a good job. Even more rarely do politicians learn that individual believers have been praying for them. And yet, this is precisely Paul's command. "First of all, then, I urge that entreaties and prayers, petitions and thanksgivings, be made on behalf of all men, for kings and all who are in authority, in order that we may lead a tranquil and quiet life in all godliness and dignity" (1 Timothy 2:1-2).

Paul uses four words to stress our intercession for government leaders. We must have *entreaties* (praying for specific needs); *prayers* (a more general word referring to the need for wisdom in daily decisions); *petitions* (a reference to our ability as believers to come before God in behalf of others) and finally *thankfulness* (gratitude to God for what leadership has been provided).

Because our political leaders are often non-Christians it is easy to think there is no use praying for them. But Paul makes it clear the Christian has a duty to pray that the state will protect its citizens and encourage an atmosphere where man can be saved and come to the knowledge of the truth. If we are not constantly in prayer for our leaders we really cannot complain when our freedoms are taken away from us.

Think of what it would mean to a politician to receive letters from Christians without complaints, just to say that they are praying. With such power at our disposal we might be surprised at what God would bring about simply because His people are obedient to this command.

Submission

When Paul wrote the book of Romans, Christianity was not viewed with favor in the Roman Empire. Yet he exalts the role of government in the economy of God, and says, "Let every person be in subjection to the governing authorities. For there is no authority except from God, and those which exist are established by God. Therefore he who resists authority has opposed the ordinance of God; and they who have opposed will receive condemnation upon themselves" (Romans 13:1-2).

Why does Paul urge submission? First, because government is ordained of God. This is difficult to believe, particularly when we see the evil governments in existence today. What about China? The Soviet Union? Iran or Libya?

The Scriptures teach an interesting paradox: On the one hand Satan is actively involved in the political process. In fact, he said to Christ " 'I will give you all this domain and its glory; for it has been handed over to me, and I give it to whomsoever I wish. Therefore if you worship before me it shall all be yours' " (Luke 4:6-7). The book of Daniel teaches that there are wicked spirits who are assigned to various leaders. There is no question that some world leaders are but tools of the devil.

Yet at the same time the Bible clearly teaches that God rules in the affairs of men. "For not from the east, nor from the west, nor from the desert comes exaltation; but God is the judge; He puts down one, and exalts another" (Psalm 75:6-7).

Even more vividly, Nebuchadnezzar was driven to

insanity and ate grass like the cattle until he learned that "The Most High is ruler over the realm of mankind, and bestows it on whomever He wishes" (Daniel 4:25*b*).

How shall we understand this apparent contradiction? Satan's authority is *derived*, it is not inherent in his own person. God has given him the rulership of the world, but he exercises his authority within the limitations prescribed by God. God controls the ultimate outcome of whatever decisions Satan may be allowed to make. And, of course, God rules everything according to His own will and to accomplish His own ultimate purpose. Yes, Nero along with Hitler and Stalin were "ordained of God."

Furthermore, government *represents* God. Paul wrote, "Therefore he who resists authority has opposed the ordinance of God; and they who have opposed will receive condemnation upon themselves." To resist governmental authority is to resist God. Whether we think a law is fair or not, we have no right to disobey simply because of our own preferences. Government is God-ordained.

But should we always obey the government? No, not always. As we shall see in the final chapter of this book, there is a place for civil disobedience. The history of the Christian church is filled with names of those who believed that they must obey God and not the rules of men.

INVOLVEMENT

In the early days of America Christians took leadership in the government without any thought that Christianity and politics might not mix. Only after the modernist-fundamentalist controversy did fundamentalism withdraw from the political arena. The notion that Christians should not be involved in government has given the secularists a grand opportunity to entrench themselves in the political process. Thankfully, the situation is changing as Christians become more aware of their responsibility toward God in government. Senator Mark Hatfield wrote:

> For the Christian man to reason that God does not want him in politics because there are too many evil men in government is as insensitive as for a Christian doctor to turn his back on an epidemic because there are too many germs there . . . For the Christian to say he will not enter politics because he might lose his faith is the same as for a physician to say that he will not heal men because he might catch their disease.[1]

We must agree with Daniel Webster that "whatever makes men good Christians makes them good citizens." As individuals we can be a part of the political process without identifying the Christian church as officially supporting a given political party. In politics we must fight for the candidates who come the closest to the ideals that we hold while recognizing that no one may agree with us on every issue.

Some Christians can become directly involved in the political process. Campaigns succeed only because there are many people who make them succeed. Christians have an opportunity to support their candidate and to make sure that he will be elected.

Every single Christian can make his views known to state and federal representatives. Letters, phone calls, and the media can all be used to let the world know that we will not be intimidated by the smothering voice of the secularists. The fact that church-state issues have been discussed by the media in recent years is a good sign. It is an indication that the public

1. Quoted in John Eidsmoe, *God and Caesar* (Westchester, Ill.: Crossway, 1984), p. 57.

is becoming aware of the existence of religious groups that are using the political process to highlight the importance of moral issues.

Finally, let's not minimize the need to be salt and light in our families, neighborhoods, and vocations. When Abraham pled with God not to overthrow Sodom and Gomorrah as long as ten righteous still lived in the city, God granted the request. Abraham had evidently overestimated the number of righteous, but God graciously removed His people before the judgment came. Similarly, we cannot exempt ourselves from the people who live next door to us. When judgment comes to a nation it falls on the righteous as well as the unrighteous. It is our responsibility to use all the leverage we can to preserve our freedoms and to stay God's hand of judgment.

The time might come when our freedoms will be taken away from us. But until then we must be involved in government at every level.

The Moral Majority

Back in 1965 the Reverend Jerry Falwell stated that he would never stop preaching the pure saving gospel of Christ to do anything else, including fighting Communism or participating in civil rights reforms. He believed that preachers were not called to be politicians but to be soul winners. Nowhere in the Bible are we commanded to reform the externals.

Yet today Falwell believes he was in error. In 1978 he founded a group called the Moral Majority, a political bloc that seeks to elect candidates who have biblical values. In the process, he now finds himself linked to those whose theology differs sharply from his fundamentalism. The reason is because politics depends on numbers. The political game has always been played by the deft art of compromise—you must reach out across ideological barriers for the sake of shared goals. So Falwell the fundamentalist now joins hands with Catholics, Jews, and Mormons. Tim La-Haye, founder of a similar group (The American Coalition for Traditional Values), recently found himself attending a function in support of the Unification Church because he believed it had experienced discrimination. As has often been observed, politics makes strange bedfellows.

Of course neither Falwell nor LaHaye would admit to compromise. They point out, quite correctly, that they have not surrendered a single doctrinal distinctive. *Political cooperation is not theological cooperation.*

This approach to political alignment received credibility through the writings of the late Francis Schaeffer. He spoke about the need for cobelligerency, that Christians should cooperate with those who have different religious views to attain some political or social goals. If a water main were broken along a street, it would not matter whether your next door neighbor was a Mormon or an atheist; you would band together to get city hall to restore the water service. If we can cooperate on that level without doctrinal compromise, why can't Christians join hands with others to fight abortion, gay liberation, and even the nuclear freeze?

Historians tell us that such cobelligerency is unprecedented in church history. The New Testament teaches submission to governmental authority without any hint that the church should change society through uniting in a political organization. Although Christians have always been individually involved in politics, this is the first time a separate political organization has been formed under the banner of fundamental Christianity. However, the American political process invites such participation. Given the uniqueness of our political system it is not surprising that there are no other clear examples of such involvement.

As already indicated, we can be grateful for every Christian in politics. We ought to support organizations that attempt to educate the religious constituency of the issues debated in Washington. Christians ought to make their influence felt in local as well as national elections and speak up for what they believe. Often we have lost crucial battles by default.

But there are subtle dangers involved in organized cobelligerency. The first is that biblical and political issues tend to be mixed together as part of one lump. Abortion is a biblical issue—we can all unite in our opposition to the arbitrary killing of human life. But what about the need for a stronger defense, the MX missile for example? Christians have every right to disagree on such matters. Some say we should not give the impression that our armaments will keep us from falling into the hands of the Soviets. We of all people should know what may have escaped the attention of the Pentagon: regardless of its military might, any nation can fall if it does not repent of its sin.

The city of Babylon was justifiably considered impregnable. It was captured not because it lacked solid defenses but because God weighed it on His scale and found righteousness wanting. Our message as Christians must be clear: repent, or judgment of some kind is inevitable, a huge defense budget notwithstanding. Let's distinguish between primary issues in which we all must be united and those secondary matters where differences of opinion may well exist.

A second danger is that political reformation could subtly substitute for spiritual transformation. Of course we all favor laws that reflect biblical morality. But such progress falls far short of the real answer to our national decay.

Suppose prayer is restored to our public schools. Because of our pluralistic society, such prayers might be based on the lowest common denominator of all religions. Even a period of silence in which children may meditate or pray could be misused by teachers bent on rebelling against a religious emphasis forced on them.

I favor teaching creationism in our public schools as an alternate explanation of origins. Yet this would hardly make us a Christian nation. Whatever lip service we achieve through such laws would fall far short of the change of heart God desires. We may honor God with our lips, but our heart is far from Him. We know that the law cannot save an individual; it cannot save a country either.

Third, the purity of the Christian message can easily be lost when we identify with non-Christian groups with whom we strongly disagree on all spiritual issues except that they happen to share common social concerns. With the cooperation of Catholics, Jews, and Mormons, it would be easy for the uninformed to assume that all of those who cooperate with the Moral Majority believe the same theologically. As Randy Frame puts it, "For cobelligerency means two human beings side by side, waging a common struggle, rejoicing together in victory and weeping together in defeat. This relationship can make it extremely difficult for one to maintain his theological convictions if so doing entails believing that his comrade is ultimately disillusioned and bound for hell."[2]

Even more importantly, *when we identify God with any political party we might find we are unable to speak the Word of God to both parties.* We cannot sell our soul to either the Democrats or the Republicans since we must be able to say to both of them "Repent!" In a fallen world no one party is all right and the other all wrong.

Finally, what if we simply do not have the political

2. Randy Frame, "Strange Bedfellows," *Eternity,* January 1985, pp. 21-22.

power to bring about reform? Yes, we are winning some battles and we might continue to do so. But our gains are dependent on the ballot box. Someone has said, "The art of politics is the art of destroying your enemies." But what if our enemies outnumber us? This in itself should not deter us from striving for our objectives, but we must remember that ultimately the fate of our nation depends on its relationship to the living God. *We cannot apply a political solution to what is essentially a spiritual problem.*

Despite these dangers we can be thankful for groups such as the Moral Majority, which have inspired Christians to become active in politics. History may record that it was the participation of Christians in politics in the 1980s that awakened this nation from its slide into the abyss of moral oblivion. Nazism triumphed in Germany, at least in part, because the church voiced little opposition to Hitler's brazen political methods and calloused moral behavior. This cannot be said of the church in America. Because of the writings of Francis Schaeffer and the preaching of men like Jerry Falwell, believers in the United States are better informed about what is happening all around us.

As someone has observed, a just law cannot cause whites to love blacks; nor can it cause a mother to love her child. But a law *can* protect minorities and children from abuse and murder. A law *can* guarantee freedom and constitutional protection.

May God help us to not abandon politics but to become involved so that we can help bring justice to our ailing society.

11

THE MYTH THAT
WE CAN TAKE ON WATER
AND STAY AFLOAT

The church is to be in the world as a ship is in the ocean. We are to be *in* the world but not *of* it. But the evangelical ship is taking on water. The world is seeping into the church so rapidly that the vessel is in danger of being submerged. The church, which is to influence the world, finds herself powerfully influenced *by* the world. Remember the boy who put a sparrow in the same cage as a canary, hoping that the bird would learn to sing? But later he remarked disappointedly, "The sparrow doesn't sound like a canary, but the canary sounds like a sparrow!"

If we as Christ's representatives can scarcely stay afloat because of the impact of the world, how can we have the strength to rescue the society that is sinking around us? Perhaps the greatest myth is the notion that the church can be inundated by worldly values and yet meet its responsibility of keeping society from decay. If our assignment is to reclaim the moral ground of this nation for righteousness, how can we do it if we ourselves are guilty of the same sins? To change the analogy slightly: It's hard to build a dam when you're flowing down the river!

We can be thankful for the gains we have made in making our beliefs known. The Moral Majority can point to some victories, and prolife groups can take credit for educating millions of Americans about the realities of abortion. Christian activists have helped this nation swing toward the right as seen in the last two presidential elections. But I am afraid that our gains are empty unless we get our own house in order.

Recent Gallup polls have uncovered conflicting trends in our society. Religion is on the upswing, but so are crime and immorality. The late George Gallup called it a giant paradox that religion is showing clear signs of revival even as the country is ridden with a rising crime rate and other problems that are regarded as antithetical to religious piety. Addressing a national seminar of Southern Baptist leaders, Gallup said that there is very little difference in the ethical behavior between churchgoers and those who are not active religiously—the levels of lying, cheating, and stealing are remarkably the same in both groups. What an indictment of American Christianity to have religion up while morality is down! Let's not excuse ourselves or the results of polls because we suspect that the majority of those interviewed were not born-again Christians. Within evangelicalism there is a distressing drift toward accepting a Christianity that does not demand a life-changing walk with God.

Like the nominally religious, we choose what we will believe and how we will act without much concern for what the Bible teaches. Carl F. H. Henry wrote, "Millions of Protestants, many evangelicals among them, choose and change their churches as they do their airlines—for convenience of travel, comfort and economy."[1]

History has shown that the church has always had its greatest impact on the world during difficult times, not when Christianity was popular. When Constantine became emperor and made Christianity the official religion of the Roman Empire in A.D. 313, Christians were, understandably, relieved. Considering all the persecution they had gone through, we can understand why the majority welcomed the change of political climate. But genuine Christianity declined, and dead ritualism became the order of the day. Christianity absorbed the culture around it and gone was its spontaneity and vibrancy. Tertullian observed that Christianity needed persecution to survive.

Evangelicalism, often thought to belong to the fringes of the main stream of religion, has become popular in America. As Richard J. Mouw said, "During the past one hundred years the evangelical witness has regularly been viewed as the dying gasp of an endangered species."[2] But today the born-again movement has become popular and thus many have felt free to identify with it at no personal cost. The stigma of Christianity is gone, but so is its power. As Martin Marty said in an interview in the *Los Angeles Herald-Examiner*, "Today you can't say turning to Jesus means you are turning your back on the world."

Can evangelicalism survive its popularity? Jon Johnson in a book on this topic argues that we have received a clean bill of health from the world, yet our influence is far less than our numbers would suggest. He says, "The world has taken a step in our direction

1. Carl F. H. Henry, *The Christian Mindset in a Secular Society* (Portland, Ore.: Multnomah, 1984), p. 33.
2. Richard J. Mouw, "Evangelicals in Search of Maturity," *Theology Today*, April 1978, p. 42.

and we have responded by scrambling to its presence."[3] Someone has quipped that too many Christians pride themselves in being "trendier than thou."

When the media tells us that mothers should pursue
a career outside the home, we restudy our Bibles and
discover that yes, this is perfectly acceptable for
Christian women, too. When the homosexual community tells us that the Bible does not condemn those who
are homosexuals by orientation, some evangelicals
resort to novel interpretations and conclude that we
have in fact misinterpreted Paul. And when the pre-
vailing mood is toward a belief in a Marxist theory of
the redistribution of wealth, some evangelicals jump
on that bandwagon, too. This is not to say that we
should not restudy the Bible to see its relevance to our
society. But there is something suspicious about evangelicalism when it turns its sail with every wind that
blows. When we accommodate the Scripture in a desire to be relevant, we have nothing to say to this
generation.

In *The Great Evangelical Disaster* Francis Schaeffer
says, "Here is the great evangelical disaster—the failure of the evangelical world to stand for truth as
truth . . . the evangelical church has accommodat-
ed to the world spirit of the age."[4] Little wonder we
are being overrun by the cults, inundated with pornography, and destroyed by abortion on demand.

THE RESPONSIBILITY OF THE CHURCH

It is popular to blame the Supreme Court, the humanists, and radical feminists for the loss of our freedoms and the moral declension of our country. To be

3. Jon Johnson, *Will Evangelicalism Survive Its Own Popularity?* (Grand
   Rapids: Zondervan, 1980), p. 37.
4. Francis Schaeffer, *The Great Evangelical Disaster* (Westchester, Ill.:
   Crossway, 1984), p. 37.

sure they have all done their part in eroding standards of decency and encouraging a disrespect for
human life. But if God is using them to judge us, might
not the responsibility be more properly laid at the feet
of those who know the living God but have failed to
influence society?

As already implied, if we were few in number, we
could more easily evade censure, but there are tens
of thousands of evangelical congregations in America representing several million born-again believers.
And yet we continue to lose crucial battles. Perhaps
the church does not suffer for the sins of the world as
much as the world suffers for the sins of the church.

I don't know how many times I've heard that God is
going to have to judge America because she has
sinned against so much light. The impression given is
that God is overlooking our sins for the present, but
intends to make up for lost time in the distant future. Of
course, it may well be that God will bring a cata-
strophic judgment to America—a war with Russia,
famine, or maybe He will allow the nation to be under
the control of an atheistic government, such as in
Communist countries. But the nature of sin is such that
it is always accompanied by *immediate* judgment.

Sin, if unconfessed, must have consequences the
moment it is committed. And for our sins we are already paying the utmost farthing. God is allowing
Satan to fragment our families, to bring emotional
and spiritual devastation to our children through divorce and immorality. *The church today is buffeted
by the severe discipline of God, and doesn't even
know it!*

How can we explain that there are as many divorces within the church as outside it? What about
Gallup's observation that the behavior of the religious
and the nonreligious is indistinguishable? Why is it
that so many Christian leaders are falling into the sin

of immorality? Certainly it is not because Satan is more powerful than he was in the past, or that he is increasing in wickedness. Rather, it must be because he has been given more authority as God disciplines the church. Disobedience exposes us to the whims and wiles of the devil.

God judged Israel by withdrawing His presence. Read carefully His own words, "Then My anger will be kindled against them in that day, and I will forsake them and hide My face from them, and they shall be consumed, and many evils and troubles shall come upon them; so that they will say in that day, 'Is it not because our God is not among us that these evils have come upon us?' " (Deuteronomy 31:17). What form did that discipline take? After He warned the Israelites of famines, wars, and boils, He predicted that the final judgment would be the breakup of the families. "Your sons and your daughters shall be given to another people, while your eyes shall look on and yearn for them continually; but there shall be nothing you can do" (Deuteronomy 28:32). The severest judgment was the scattering of Israel's families.

Though in a different way, the same thing is happening in America today. One half of all children born this year will live with only a single parent, and the statistics within the church are not much better. The emotional scars left on our children will be passed on to the next generation. Bitterness, hatred, rejection—all these and more are the legacy for our sins.

God's judgment will also include intensifying emotional disorders. He said the Israelites' disobedience would bring "despair of soul" (Deuteronomy 28:65). Unresolved guilt and rejection often surface under different labels such as anger, insensitivity, and depression. With millions of women having abortions and an equal number of men guilty of sexual immorality, fu-

ture generations will find mental illness on the increase. We are rotting from within.

And how have we contributed to this national mental breakdown? Simply stated, *we are guilty of the
same sins as the world.* When we adopt the same
values and conduct as the world, as already stated,
we take ourselves out from under the protection of
God. When we are in Satan's territory, he is free to
harass and to control the people of God. Only this can
explain why Christian wives are leaving their husbands to "find themselves," and Christian husbands
are abandoning their wives and children to seek
some elusive dream.

Just recently a distraught husband told me that his
wife has, in the past few months, turned into "another
person." Though she adored her husband for more
than ten years, she now says that she never did love
him. Her demands have become so irrational that
there is no use even trying to reason with her. How did
this come about? First of all, she became friends with
a feminist who convinced her that she was being
treated unfairly. It wasn't right that she should have to
stay home to rear children; after all, she had as much
a right to her career as did her husband to his. She
should have turned away from the counsel of the
wicked and if necessary cut off all association with
her so-called friend. The book of Proverbs is filled with
warnings about listening to wrong counsel and the
need to walk away from those who intend to lead us
astray. Second, she as a mother was working outside
the home. Because of this disobedience, God was no
longer obligated to protect her from the wiles of the
devil. While at work, she met another man who was
more understanding than her husband, and in her
words "really meets my needs." So she broke up the
marriage. The children have been damaged emotionally and may never recover, but it makes little

difference. After all, you only live once, and you have to look out for Number 1.

Part of the reason for such behavior is that all the social restraints that once discouraged women from divorce are now gone. Divorce is not only socially acceptable, but staying married to the same man is to some rather mindless—especially if a woman thinks she can make a better life with someone else.

Just as God sent a wicked spirit to trouble Saul as a judgment for his jealousy, so God, I believe, sends wicked spirits to discipline His people. This probably explains why my friend's wife is "a different person." God's intention, of course, is that she would be brought to repentance. Through an intensification of depression and guilt, God's desire would be that she might become so miserable that she would turn from her error. But regardless of how much emotional turbulence she experiences, she is able to rationalize it away. Meanwhile, the price for disobedience is being paid in her own heart and in the lives of her children and husband. There is no use waiting for God's discipline at some future time. It's happening before our eyes.

Recently I heard of another pastor who fell into the sin of immorality. How did it begin? Through counseling sessions he had with women. But where does the Bible teach that a man should counsel a woman if she has problems in her marriage? Paul taught that the older women are to teach the young women to "love their husbands, to love their children" (Titus 2:4). This is another reminder that when we trust our own wisdom we risk the possibility of sinning and hence attracting the discipline of God.

WHY WE LOSE BATTLES

Historians agree that it is difficult to pinpoint the cause-effect relationships in church history. We cannot always say with certainty why the church went through a time of persecution during one era and then experienced relative peace with political authorities in the next.

But there is a story in the Old Testament that proves that secular man is not able to find the root cause of society's ills. It also shows the consequences of hidden sin.

Give this some thought: suppose you were responsible for a military campaign and you lost a battle decisively. What would you look for in analyzing the cause of the defeat? Probably you would find out if you had enough men, if you used the right strategy, or if you had defective equipment. But incredibly in the story found in Joshua 7, these matters had nothing to do with the defeat. God says it was because a man stole a coat and some gold and silver and then hid them in his tent.

What a startling analysis. What possible relationship could there be between some stolen goods and a defeat on the battlefield? Though humanly speaking there is no discernible relationship between petty theft and the outcome of a battle, the disobedience of one man caused the death of thirty-six others. The lesson to be learned is that you cannot control the consequences of sin. God operates outside of the normal cause-effect relationships.

Achan coveted and then he stole. He tolerated one sin and then had to accept another. Just as guilt may come to the surface as depression or anger, so any individual sin can sprout in all kinds of different directions. To put it simply, you cannot be victorious in one area of your life if you are tolerating sin in another. The consequences of sin are haphazard and unpredictable.

But there is more to the story. In Joshua 7:1 we read, "But the sons of Israel acted unfaithfully in regard to the things under the ban." If I had been from the tribe of Simeon, I would have objected, "That's not fair—I wasn't involved in the sin of stealing. Why is God blaming all the rest of us?" Whether we like it or not, God has ordained that there be solidarity among people. There is the principle of shared guilt. In Exodus the Lord said that He visits the iniquity of the fathers upon the children to the third and fourth generation.

How does all this relate to the church? Paul says that when one part of the Body suffers the whole Body suffers with it. When one member of the church harbors sin, the whole Body is affected. A little cold water poured into a container lowers the temperature of whole; conversely hot water will raise the temperature. Thus the spiritual life of every individual Christian affects the total Body of Christ either negatively or positively. Either you are helping or you are a burden, a dead weight that someone else must carry.

When God instructed Joshua to find the culprit by casting lots, Achan would not admit to his sin until the lot fell on him. The fear and shame connected with the whole affair made him hold out as long as possible. Every moment of misery was more attractive to him than the shame of exposure. When he was judged, members of his family were stoned with him, possibly because they cooperated with him in knowing that the items were hidden in the tent.

But what would happen if believers in America would be willing to expose the Achans among us? What if we were willing to confess our sins collectively, knowing that as a body we are all related? What if we fearlessly exposed sin when it is brought to light?

Undoubtedly, God deals differently with the church than He did with Israel. But if Israel lost thirty-six men on the battlefield because of the hidden sin of one man, *it is conceivable* that God might give us as the church the wisdom and strength needed to save this nation if we are willing to take sin seriously and be a pure church in the midst of a sinful society.

Survival Through Repentance

Where then have we failed? If the church is serious about returning to God's protection, it must place itself under His authority. Here are some areas of compromise that we should consider.

1. *We have accepted divorce as an option to resolve the difficulties in our marriages.*

Yes, we are all tragically aware of those difficult situations in which reconciliation appears to be out of the question. As a pastor, I have seen my share of couples whose problems defy solutions. Often there are those who do not wish to have a divorce, but their partner has walked out on them. As a church we must proclaim the permanency of marriage, but also deal redemptively with those who are the tragic victims of divorce.

But the majority of divorces among believers could be avoided, indeed *all* could be, if we bowed to the authority of the Scriptures and brought the resources of Christ to bear on the marriage. Whenever a divorce takes place, God is trying to get our attention. It's time to fast and pray that Satan's power might be broken.

What do we have to say to the world if Christ is unable to bring happiness to Christian marriages? Every couple that divorces causes others within and without the church to question the power of the message we preach. We must repent of our rebellion, worldly values, and hardness of heart.

2. *We have accepted the world's philosophy that mothers should have their own career outside the home.*

We have already noticed that the policy in Communist countries is that women should work so that the state can rear the children. But the Bible teaches that mothers are to stay home to care for their children. But the pressure of the world is so great that it is easy for us to think that we need two incomes; or worse, that a mother has the right to find fulfillment in a career outside the home. Actually, her responsibility in rearing children is an honor that no one else should take from her. Of all that we have in this world, only our children can be taken to heaven with us.

I am well aware that husbands have not always given their wives the place of honor, and the failure of men must be pointed out. However, many Christians have simply ignored God's instructions and have blindly followed their own desires. We cannot have strong churches without strong homes.

3. *We have accepted the world's entertainment, leisure, and values.*

If the polls are correct, Christians and non-Christians have about the same kinds of entertainment and priorities. Many Christians are caught in the vice of pornography and the love of leisure. This accounts for many of the problems in our homes.

Along with this is the sin of materialism. We have often heard people say, "Well you've got to earn a living." However, often such a remark is used as an excuse to sell ourselves to the greed of this world. The love of money has made us give first-rate priorities to second-rate causes. The new "God wants you to be rich, happy, and healthy" philosophy has appealed to a generation that is quick to accept the benefits of Christianity without painful obedience. Like a child standing by a slot machine hoping he can win the jackpot with a single coin, many Christians expect maximum return for minimum commitment. When such believers are not healed or do not get a promotion, they take their quarter and go somewhere else.

4. *We have treated the unconverted with benign neglect.*

Many Christians have never made a concerted effort to witness to the saving power of Christ. Of course it's difficult to share from a life crammed full of besetting sins and pleasure. As one person put it, "I am like a cup trying desperately to spill over." Having spoiled our appetite for God by nibbling at the world, we have little to share with our neighbors.

We have bought the devil's lie that the world does not want to hear the gospel. But behind the facade of pleasure and the excitement of getting ahead in the world are numerous empty and disillusioned people seeking for the missing piece of life's puzzle. Yet often we have not taken the time to wait before the Lord until we are burdened for our part of the world. Although we may claim to believe in hell, no one would guess it by our silent lips.

5. *We have become too narrow in our vision.*

It's so easy to believe that if God is going to do a mighty work, it must be done through our particular church or denomination. Let's remember that Christ said, "Upon this rock I will build My church." The word *church* is singular, not plural. Whereas it is important to maintain fundamental doctrinal distinctives, we must also recognize that God often uses those who do not agree with us.

Two men spent an afternoon fishing. One of them kept throwing the big trout back into the lake, keeping only the small ones. His partner was puzzled and asked about this curious practice. "I've only got an 8-inch frying pan at home," was the reply. So it is with us. God may want to give us special blessings, but if they do not fit our special box we toss them aside.

No doubt a return to biblical teaching will be resisted by many of our pleasure-loving churches. But if we want to win the battle, we had better know *that we cannot do it unless God takes up our cause.* The only hope for America can be found in the church. The Body of Christ still wields awesome power. If we are brought to our knees, God may begin to give us spiritual victories that could stem abortion, infanticide, and drug abuse. If it is true that the visibility of evangelicals has not translated into moral and political strength, it might well be because the church and the world no longer see one another as enemies but have become friends. It is our responsibility to realize that every concession weakens us. There's no such thing as a compromise that will ever give us strength.

I fear we are losing our ability to rescue the world around us because we ourselves are going under. If we want to stay afloat, we have to accept once again the kind of Christianity that cannot tolerate the world.

When Stephen Olford was asked regarding the secret of a powerful ministry he replied that the characteristics of a church should be bent knees, broken hearts, and wet eyes.

God is not obligated to spare us persecution even if we should repent. But He may. If society were transformed by the active witness of believers, our freedoms might remain intact.

At least we could speak to the world with the authority of God. Apart from that we are sure to lose the battle.

12

THE MYTH THAT
WE CAN WIN THE WAR
WITHOUT SACRIFICE

During one of his many polar expeditions, Rear Admiral Robert Peary headed north with one of his dog teams. At the end of the day when he stopped to take a bearing on his latitude, he was amazed to discover that he actually was farther south than he had been at the beginning of the day.

The mystery was eventually solved when he found that he had been traveling on a gigantic ice flow. Ocean currents were pulling it south faster than the dog teams could drive north.

We have all felt that way. As a church we work hard, only to discover that we are losing ground. Our activity does not always produce the results we would like to see. The momentum does not seem to be with us.

Why?

I fear we are not yet at the place where we are willing to sacrifice; we are a people with many preferences but few convictions.

According to attorney David Gibbs, who has been

involved with disputes regarding private schools, in 1972 the Supreme Court clarified the difference between a conviction and a preference. After all, it is religious convictions and not preferences that are protected by the Constitution. How did the Court decide to tell the difference? Gibbs summarized the conclusions of the Court: A conviction was a religious belief that was believed to be God-given, *therefore it would never change under any circumstances.* Anything less was merely a religious preference.

Thus in solving the question of whether parents actually had a conviction that their children should not attend a public school, the questioning in the courtroom would sound like this:

Prosecuting Attorney: Do you approve of adultery and profanity?

Defendant: No.

Prosecuting Attorney: Do you have a television set in your home?

Defendant: Yes.

Prosecuting Attorney: Have you ever seen adulterous scenes and heard profanity on it?

Defendant: Yes.

Prosecuting Attorney: Then it is obvious that you have only a religious preference about these matters . . . if you held these beliefs as convictions you would not have a television set in your home.

Gibbs gives the Amish man Mr. Yoder as an example of someone who had religious conviction about not sending his children to public schools. Yoder was told that he would be fined for breaking the law, but he refused to be intimidated. Finally he was put in jail by authorities who believed that this would force him to recant his position. But he would not bend. When his case was taken to the Supreme Court it agreed that he did not have to send his children to a public school because he had proved that he held his belief as a religious conviction and not just a preference.

Given such an understanding of religious convictions, we can see evangelicalism in America is rife with religious preferences but few convictions. Though we speak loudly about our many beliefs, there are precious few matters that we hold so dear that we would be willing to go to jail for them. Most issues that we profess to believe are up for grabs, to be sold to the highest bidder.

Neither the world nor the devil will take notice until we are ready to draw the line and stick with our convictions whatever the cost.

Perhaps the reason we will lose the battle against secularism is that our spirit is willing, but our flesh is weak. Jerry Mander observed, "I'm learning that people can hate a lot of television, hate their own viewing habits, hate what it does to them and their families and still think it bizarre that anyone wants to get rid of it." Lots of preferences, no convictions.

In order to press ahead in the preservation of our freedoms, we must think through a theology of (1) *penetration,* (2) *confrontation,* and (3) *survival.* Only then are we ready for the battle ahead.

A THEOLOGY OF PENETRATION

Solzhenitsyn believes it may be too late for us to turn the tide in America. But he adds, "It is better to fight from one's knees than not at all." This is not the time to retreat into an evangelical cocoon waiting for the final judgment. In whatever time we have left, we must *act.*

Salt and light are the two metaphors Christ used to describe His children in the world. Salt is known as a preservative; it is used to keep meat from decay. This implies that the earth is rotten, sin has made our planet polluted and a moral cesspool. Believers keep it from total disintegration.

Imagine what the world would say if we told it that Christians are restraining society from total moral collapse. The world thinks just the opposite. It views Christianity as an obstacle to moral progress. The Bible is seen as an outdated collection of opinions that deserve derision rather than respect. Yet Christ's words are best translated, "Ye and ye alone are the salt of the earth." The earth has a debt to Christianity that it does not realize. Salt is used primarily to prevent putrification; it is an antiseptic that slows the process of decay. Proportionately, little salt is needed in comparison to the weight of meat.

But of course salt must be in contact with decaying meat to be effective. We cannot retreat to monasteries as the monks did in medieval times, nor can we hide behind our piety.

If I could pinpoint the reason for our lack of influence in the world, it might be simply this: *We as individuals are unwilling to be salt right where we are.* Many of us are intimidated by the world. A Christian nurse will help perform abortions, rationalizing her stance by saying that the baby would have been aborted anyway; what is more, her job is on the line. Those who stand against abortion are treated condescendingly and with pity because they are out of step with the times. So many Christians succumb to the culture around them rather than stand against it.

Every one of us longs for someone to do something about abortion. But we prefer it be done by the Catholics, or by Jerry Falwell. We are unwilling to become personally involved. And because of that, our impact in society is lessened.

Christ spoke about the salt that had lost its savor. It was worthless, to be cast out. Perhaps it became polluted, mixed with impurities. This is an apt description of the state of the church today. *Our greatest problem may not be secular humanism but the secularization of the church itself.* With millions of believers who care little about serious Bible study or intercessory prayer, it is not surprising that we are unable to keep society from decay even though there are more believers in America proportionately than in any other country of the world. Theoretically we have enough salt, it's just that it seems to be getting as soiled as the meat it's supposed to preserve.

Christians should be attending PTA meetings, becoming active in a community's decision-making process, and meeting with local and public school libraries to make our preferences known. We are the ones who should be encouraging our state and federal representatives and letting them know where we stand on the issues. We should be speaking out through writing, television, and individual discussions about what is happening in our country. We cannot be salt if we become indistinguishable from the meat.

Light is the next figure of speech our Lord used. Again, the imagery suggests that the world is in darkness. Ironically, the world thinks its wisdom is light. But however much knowledge men have, they lack wisdom—insight into the moral and spiritual affairs of mankind. Never in history has so much advice been available on marriage, guilt, child rearing, and personal relationships in general. Yet along with this explosion of knowledge we have more family breakups, child abuse, and neurosis than at any other time in history. Even the humanists, who gave us the "if-it-feels-good-do-it" philosophy, at times admit we have gone too far.

In reality the world does not have any idea how to avoid evil; how to live in clean and wholesome ways. No one can bring light to the world except the Christian.

Christ says that we must not hide our light but let it shine, so that the world "may see your good works, and glorify your Father who is in heaven" (Matthew 5:16). The end result is to lead others to faith in Christ. How else could the world glorify God?

Christian teachers, sensitive to the restrictions placed on them by the courts, are tempted to hide their light under a bushel. They can easily deny Christ by their silence. If the present trend continues, we know that it will become increasingly difficult to witness openly about Christ in our classrooms or anywhere for that matter. Are we creatively thinking of ways to share the gospel in an environment that seeks to confine religion within the walls of a church, temple, or synagogue? A bright light shining in a desert is worthless; what we need is a light that points the way. We must not only live the Christian life but speak it so that men and women can come to know Christ.

We can be thankful for our new visibility as evangelicals, *but popularity is not a substitute for influence.* And although we are thankful for the many organizations that are promoting traditional values, we cannot expect them to do it without the active support and involvement of every single believer.

We cannot expect the Christian media to do our job for us. The message of Christ must come to this world wrapped in a warm body. Seldom do people receive Christ as Savior simply because they have heard the message; they must have it personally explained by someone who *lives* the message. That's why the early church captured so much of the world of its day. It was not through the media, obviously—it was because every believer was actively sharing the gospel.

In his book *A Severe Mercy* Sheldon Vanauken talks about his first encounter with Christians. That night he wrote these words in his diary:

> The best argument for Christianity is Christians, their joy, their certainty, their completeness. But the strongest argument *against* Christianity is also Christians—when they are somber and joyless, when they are self-righteous and smug in complacent consecration, when they are narrow and repressive, then Christianity dies a thousand deaths . . . indeed there are impressive indications that the positive quality of joy is in Christianity—and possibly no where else. If that were certain, it would be proof of a very high order.[1]

Could every individual in America be personally confronted with the saving message of Christ? Yes, if we were to follow this simple plan: if every believer were to list six people—two from his family or relatives, two from his neighborhood, two from his place of work—and then pray and strategize as to how these may be led to Christ. We have the numbers to confront the majority of Americans with a loving presentation of the gospel. Nothing would change public opinion more quickly than the conversion of millions of Americans.

But if salt has lost its savor, and our light is effectively hidden, we can expect the decay to increase.

If every Christian were as committed as you, how great would our impact be?

A THEOLOGY OF CONFRONTATION

Until now in America, Christians have assumed that they should obey the government. But the mood is changing for one good reason: when the state im-

1. Sheldon Vanauken, *A Severe Mercy* (New York: Harper & Row, 1977), p. 85.

poses a humanistic ethic on the populace, we can no longer obey its demands. As Francis Schaeffer was fond of pointing out, if you say you will *always* obey the government, then you recognize no power above the state. In other words, the state has become your god.

What about Romans 13, where Paul says we should submit to the powers that be? In context, Paul was assuming that the government was a good one. Furthermore, we must remember that there is a difference between submission and obedience. We can submit to the state by accepting the penalties that accompany our resistance, whether it be torture or jail.

Both the Bible and church history are filled with examples of those who defied authorities so that they might be obedient to God.

The midwives during the times of Moses; Daniel who prayed three times a day despite the king's decree; Shadrach, Meshach, and Abed-nego; the apostles of the New Testament—all those men believed that obedience to God superseded obedience to the state. They paid the penalty for their disobedience, but they would not violate their own consciences.

In Communist countries today, parents must disobey the state if they teach their children about God. In many places believers must assemble in small groups in defiance of state laws. And of course, sharing the faith with others is forbidden. Let us remember that in the American public schools of today religion is as forcibly excluded as it is in Russia. Humanism sees religion and absolute morality as its enemy. Thus we must become aquainted with the theology of resistance.

Are we willing to have the determination of John Bunyan? Back in seventeenth-century England, John Bunyan was told that he would have to be licensed if he continued to preach the gospel. But he knew that licensing meant control, so he went to jail instead. He had a wife and an epileptic daughter whom he dearly loved. Yet he loved Jesus more, and he knew he could not deny his calling. Apparently, his license was placed outside his cell, and if at any time he reached out and picked it up, he would be a free man. Yet he stayed in a dungeon underground that was damp and dirty, with no bed upon which to sleep. He refused to obey the state.

Bunyan had few visitors in his jail cell. His church had been boarded up, and his fellow preachers had obeyed the authority of the state. But there in prison he wrote the *Pilgrim's Progress.* The next time you read the book remember it was written by a man who refused to accept the authority of the state when it conflicted with his religious convictions.

We must think through the question of when we would defy state authority. Lynn Buzzard of the Christian Legal Society has listed issues that call into question obedience to the state.[2]

1. The state law requires immunization but parents, on religious grounds, are opposed.
2. The law of a country is opposed to religious literature, but a mission agency wants to smuggle in Bibles in fulfillment of the Great Commission.
3. Religious persons are concerned about the gross immorality of their leaders' public policy and danger to the world, and therefore want to assassinate him.
4. Blacks are prohibited from sitting near the front of the bus, but a protester wants to disregard this rule.

2. These issues were listed informally by Lynn Buzzard at the Moody Church, October 1984.

5. Where a religious person has opposition to a certain war, he chooses to resist military induction and have no part in the war.
6. A Christian who protests abortion on religious grounds refuses to pay a percentage of his income tax that would be used for federally funded abortions.
7. A church continues to keep a private school open that was ordered closed by a court because the church refuses to get a state license that it interprets as state control.
8. Parents cannot get a fair hearing regarding their views of a sex education course, and therefore they stage a sit-in the principal's office.
9. Those who believe that slavery is immoral choose to assist slaves in fleeing from their masters to safety in a free state.
10. The state law requires the taking of an oath when testifying in court, but a person disagrees with oath-taking on religious grounds.

The difficulty is, how can we determine when we should obey God and when we should obey Caesar? We may disagree on specific issues, but we must believe there is a higher law than the laws of the state. Each of us must obey God rather than man. In his book *Holy Disobedience: When Christians Must Resist the State*, Lynn Buzzard outlines seven principles to consider before taking disobedient action against the state. But he admits that he cannot give any specific answers, because that ultimately is up to the individual Christian and his own interpretation of the Bible. But regardless of what we believe on the subject, each of us should begin to think through those areas in which we are prepared to resist the state.

A helpful assignment would be to list our preferences on one side of a sheet of paper and our convictions on the other. Civil disobedience, once ignored by Christians in America, will become an increasingly important subject as America moves from its Christian base. Are we ready for such commitment?

A THEOLOGY OF SURVIVAL

Many Christians are assuming that God is obligated to come to our rescue in our conflict with the secular state. The promise of 2 Chronicles 7:14 is pressed into service to show that if the church were to repent of its sins, God would bring a revival to our land. Our freedoms would be restored, we would have righteous judges, and in short we would be both prosperous and free. But let's remember that this promise was given to Israel, not the church. In those days God explicitly told them that His chastisement was directly tied to physical blessings such as crops, drought, feast, or famine. As I write, America is having excellent crops, a thriving economy, and an optimistic view of the future. All this despite our sin.

Churches in many communist countries have gone through the fires of persecution, but God has not seen fit to deliver them from the crushing power of a humanistic state. Throughout history, God has allowed His people to chafe under the heel of hostile political authorities even when they cried to Him for deliverance. It is true of course that the number of believers in communist countries is not sufficient to reverse public policy. But even when Christians increase in number, a small humanistic elite can rule multiplied millions. China has experienced a small measure of religious freedom in recent years, but now the authorities are beginning to restrict freedom once again because they fear that religion is experiencing a comeback.

Because of the number of Christians in America,

there is a possibility that we can reverse the drift to secularism. But we cannot be sure. Perhaps God will intensify His judgment and let the forces of intolerance crush us. Since suffering has always been the earmark of the church, our turn may be around the corner.

We pray that it may not be so. But we should begin to study the churches in communist countries, to see the lessons they were forced to learn when their freedoms were taken away. For them, the state has dominated the church, so the doctrine of separation of church and state has come to mean that religion can exist in the minds of people, but cannot spill over into their life-style. Much less can it be the basis for public policy.

During the summer of 1984 my wife, children, and I had the privilege of visiting the People's Republic of China. From pastors and Christian leaders we learned firsthand what it means to live under a regime where the state attempted to stamp out religion. Space forbids an account of the persecution that the people of God endured.

Remember, the church in China survived without any help from the media—no religious radio programs, television stations, or Christian bookstores. Yet the number of believers went from less than one million in 1950 to perhaps twenty-five million today. How does the church survive when religion becomes illegal? And how can growth take place when those who are suspected of Western influence (Christianity) are hauled off to labor camps or shot to death in the presence of onlookers?

What does the church in China have to teach us?

First, the church is people, not buildings. When the word *church* is used in the New Testament it always refers to people. The Greek means "called out." It is a reference to those whom God called to Himself. When all the churches in China closed, the believers realized they would have to continue by meeting in homes. The church cannot be stamped out just because buildings are destroyed.

We in America must learn the same lesson. If our freedoms are taken away, we will be forced to discover the true nature of the church. We will not be able to hide behind a religious structure. We will have to know who we are.

Second, the church in China also teaches us that *every Christian is a minister.* As one Chinese leader told us, "I realized that we could no longer depend on the pastors or Christian leaders, so we were all forced to minister to each other." In the little house meetings, those who had no formal education had to study the Bible and assume the role of teaching. Or the person who had a Bible would read it slowly so that others could copy it. Believers would memorize Scripture together. But there was no such thing as a believer who was just going along for the ride. In a sink-or-swim atmosphere, everyone had to be committed. The church learned under pressure what we all profess to believe, namely, that God has gifted His church— there is a place for every stone in God's temple.

Third, we can see the *value of a pure church.* We were told that persecution wiped out theological liberalism. Understandably, those who had humanized Christianity had no reason to die for it. Why risk your neck for a religion that had been "demythologized?" Or why go to an early grave for a Christ who was not divine?

The church was to a great extent purified theologically, but it was also purified in other ways. In the concentration camps people were marched before a picture of Chairman Mao, and forced to bow before it twice a day. Those who did not bow had their legs broken off at the knees. Other dissenters were harassed and killed. Perhaps no church has suffered as much as that in China. But the believers who did emerge were those who were fully committed to the Lordship of Christ. Carnal Christians vanished. Persons were either fervent Communists or fervent Christians—there was no middle ground. Perhaps this explains why the church grew despite the intolerance of the state. God gave His people the grace not only to survive, but also to increase.

Finally, we learn *the attraction of joy.* According to interviews of Chinese Christians who come to Hong Kong, the reason people accepted Christianity despite the tremendous cost involved was because of the joy expressed by other believers. Under the most intense persecution, believers were able to cope much better than the millions of others who had to face the repression of a Marxist regime. Thus the authenticity of Christianity was proved. The message of the church was communicated not in word only, but also in the lives of committed believers.

When Augustine's friends heard of the fall of Rome, they hesitated to pass the news to their beloved mentor. Augustine loved the imperial city, and they knew he would be deeply hurt. But he responded by saying "Whatever men build, men will destroy . . . let's get on with building the kingdom of God."

Yes, we can give our lives to "save America," and well we might. But perhaps we can best save America by building the church, because we know that the gates of Hades will not prevail against it. Any investment we make in the church has virtually no risk because Christ has guaranteed its eventual success.

Faced as it is with the possibility of living under the intolerance of secular humanism, the church in America must have a two-pronged strategy. On the one hand we must fight from our freedom through the political process, the courts, and the media. We must stand for truth both individually and collectively regardless of the cost. But at the same time we must also not lose sight of what God is doing. He is building His church on all five continents; He is purifying His people so that they might be holy.

Someone has well said that they have no fear that the church will not succeed, but that it will succeed in those things that do not matter. We cannot allow our battle with humanism to obscure the biblical priority of the Great Commission. Evangelism and discipleship transcend any culture or political regime. I like the words of Peter Marshall, "It is better to fail in a task that will eventually succeed than to succeed in a task that will eventually fail."

The myths in this book, if widely believed, will assuredly destroy America as we know it. But the church will remain. God's purposes will be fulfilled, and believers will find the grace of God sufficient.

Whether or not God will preserve our freedoms is for Him to decide. Needless to say, we do not deserve His preservation. But if we repent and are willing to sacrifice, He may graciously spare us from the fate of millions of other believers who are ruled by the enemies of religion.

I'm not convinced that the church is desperate yet. We are largely ignorant of our true condition. We may be on the verge of learning by experience the words of William Penn, "If we are not willing to be governed by God, we shall be ruled by tyrants."

The hour is late.

Only God can save us now.